YOGA
FOR
PREGNANCY

YOGA
FOR
PREGNANCY

ROSALIND WIDDOWSON

TED SMART

Contents

Executive Editor – Jane McIntosh
Editor – Sharon Ashman
Creative Art Director – Keith Martin
Senior Designer – Claire Harvey
Book Design – J. Adams
Photography – Peter Pugh-Cooke
Production – Lucy Woodhead

First published in Great Britain in 2001
by Hamlyn, a division of
Octopus Publishing Group Limited,
2–4 Heron Quays, London E14 4JP

This edition produced for
The Book People Ltd,
Hall Wood Avenue,
Haydock,
St Helens WA11 9UL

A catalogue record for this book is
available from the British Library

Produced by Toppan Printing Company
Ltd
Printed in China

I feel particularly honoured to write this book. When I was in my teenage years, due to early medical problems, I was told that I would probably never have children. My husband Peter and I adopted a beautiful baby boy called Mark, only to find a few years later that I was pregnant, and before I knew it I was holding my darling Emily in my arms.

The Yoga practices in this book were developed during my own pregnancy and compiled in a daily diary. All my students – including the men, I'm pleased to say – joined in the development of these ideas, and I was able to teach all the way through my pregnancy until that miracle day. Of course, I have updated the practices over the years as trends have changed, but what has endured is the importance placed on caring for the mother-to-be and her baby.

The ancient yet ever-fresh science of Yoga holds out the promise of a fitter, more supple and beautiful body. Even a modest amount of practice brings renewed vitality, a notable poise and grace, confidence, improved concentration and focus, peace of mind and a sense of harmony and balance. This might seem impossible at a time when a woman can feel at her least attractive, at the mercy of processes beyond her control, and fatigued and burdened by her condition. Such a view can be changed to an entirely positive and vibrantly happy one if this period is seen as an opportunity for personal development, growth and expansion in all areas of life.

I offer you one notable observation. Through some 30 years of Yoga teaching I've noticed that 'Yoga mothers' did not seem as big as other mothers-to-be. How could this be so? Well, a well-balanced Yoga session helps with lymphatic drainage so they weren't so puffy and pudgy. They were never bothered by oedema (fluid retention) and swollen joints. They had better muscle tone so they weren't flabby. They didn't suffer so many cellulite problems because they didn't collapse into their posture and weren't prone to overweight because their endocrine system (the hormone-control system) was kept toned and healthy. They were also different in subtle ways, which one sensed, rather than saw. They exuded a poise, grace and confidence which elicited that enviable comment from others: 'You're absolutely blooming, my dear!' This was a far cry from the impression given by those unfortunate women who seemed cowed, bowed and debilitated by their oppressive condition – the fatigued and exasperated mothers-to-be who carried their pregnancy like a burden.

There are the longer-term effects, too. I am now teaching the sons and daughters of those first Yoga mothers, and it is quite striking that, even compared with their peers, these youngsters have fabulous bodies that are supple and flexible, and they appear to be more vibrant with a mental sharpness that seems absent in so many of their friends. How much is due to that early exposure in their mothers' wombs and how much to the healthy culture in which they grew up no one can state for sure. Suffice to say that this next generation of students practise their Yoga simply because they enjoy it, not because they feel they ought to do it.

When I got together with Carol Pannell, my natural childbirth expert, who collaborated on this book, there was an immediate meeting of minds. Although from different disciplines, we quickly discovered that we were talking the same language. The themes we worked with were so interrelated that we could almost have swapped classes. This most clearly demonstrated to me that there has been a fundamental shift in people's need to understand the medical and psychological basis on which the body, mind and emotions work.

In the late seventies, when I experienced my pregnancy, it was commonplace for doctors and obstetricians to recommend gentle exercise in the form of antenatal classes and they were always full. Sadly, this trend has declined and, far from being encouraged, seems to be neglected to an alarming degree. The current approach, with its fail-safe emphasis on safety, prohibits so many of these kinds of activities.

This does, however, raise the issue of what can be safely passed on to prospective students whose sole instruction comes between the covers of a book. I have therefore decided not to include a notable strand of classical Yoga practice, the inverted postures. During the potentially vulnerable period of pregnancy, these are best practised with a competent teacher who can monitor your progress, especially if you are a novice. If you are especially interested in experiencing the complete panoply that Yoga has to offer, perhaps this is your invitation and wake-up call to start attending a regular class: you will never regret following this recommendation.

Early on in the process of writing this book, I made a decision that the full range of classical Yoga postures would be rather too much for untrained pregnant women. For this work to be accessible and beneficial to the greater range of individuals, the programmes offered here have therefore been adapted to include the essence and fundamental core of posture work. At the same time my background in classical and Eastern dance has enabled me to offer a context and artform that allows for the enjoyable practice of Yoga, no matter what size you are.

It must be remembered that the wonderful art and science of Yoga has been gifted to us by great and exceptional teachers. In respect and gratitude for all I have learnt, I offer my thanks to my earliest teachers; Lettie, my Afro-Indian nanny in South Africa; B.K.S. Iyengar; Yogini Sunita; Wilfred Clark; H.H. Swami Sivananda Saraswati; Paramahansa Satyananda; my beloved Swami Tantramurti Saraswati; and every single one of my students. They have taught me so much and continue to be the very best advocates and examples of the inspiration and benefits that Yoga can bestow on all humankind.

Finally, I wish to dedicate this book to my beautiful daughter, Emily. By the very act of being nurtured in my womb, she has taught me first-hand just what is involved in the process of pregnancy and given me the joy of its finest flowering.

Rosalind Widdowson

Yoga and Pregnancy

Pregnancy is one of the three periods in a woman's life when she experiences major hormonal shifts. The first is the menarche (growth to childbearing capacity); the second is pregnancy (which also usually takes place in the early part of life); and the third is the menopause. These are all times of enormous change when the body's chemistry takes over and forces a woman to make physical, emotional and mental readjustments.

Since first pregnancy is, by and large, the preserve of young women, relatively inexperienced in life's ways, its not surprising that they have not yet developed those abilities of self-observation and regulation that is the special gift of regular Yoga practice. In fact, many young women will have had little or no experience of managing their health on a long-term basis – much to the chagrin of older women who observe the arrogance of youth with its unmarked, elastic, self-healing skin, seemingly effortless working of joints and muscles and abundant energy levels. Only later, when Nature's youthful gifts can no longer be taken for granted, do we hear the cry: 'If only I'd started younger ... ' Still, we all know how difficult it can be to sell life insurance to youngsters, or the reflective thoughtfulness that comes with experience to those zestfully revelling in and pursuing life's heady mix.

What often comes as quite a shock to newly pregnant women is the way in which they are forcibly reminded that they are hostages to the internal workings of their body systems. Some fundamental readjustments may be required if one is to accept the change from being reasonably healthy and in control of one's own health regime and lifestyle to being caught in the inexorable processes of something that is so much greater than oneself.

A physical, emotional and mental repatterning can leave women feeling stressed merely because they are not 'in control' any more and are apprehensive or even fearful because they do not know what to expect. Here, Yoga can help in a number of ways. On a physical level, it provides programmes that can actually assist the new growth and development, alleviate and dispel some of its discomforts and prevent unnecessary long-term wear and tear on the body.

Emotions during pregnancy

This new growth and development is not merely confined to the physical process of nurturing a baby. It also means taking the opportunity to appreciate a spiritual truth and expand one's horizon beyond the self-absorbed and self-orientated. A mother-to-be will, sometimes for the first time, have to put the needs of another before herself. One of my key definitions of a loving relationship is when another's wellbeing is more important than one's own. The process of pregnancy brings this truth home like no other.

On an emotional level, the breathing practices (*pranayamas*), relaxation and meditational routines that Yoga offers provide a chance to self-observe the roller-coaster of emotions and to readjust to a changing mental equilibrium. This is not so much a case of exerting 'control' to banish fear, but rather of developing an unafraid acceptance of these natural processes. Whatever your state of health, Yoga helps you to connect and flow with the natural rhythms and workings of the body. This in itself is an empowered position and does much to banish fear, stress and anxiety.

After pregnancy

Now for the *caveat* or warning. If women allow their bodies to become incapacitated during pregnancy they may never recover their bodies again – a frightening thought, and one that is often voiced in the later stages of pregnancy as women perceive their bodies ballooning out of any formerly recognized shape, and despair of ever regaining their youthful figure and lustre. If you don't want to risk having a legacy of one or more physical or emotional problems – cellulite, stretchmarks, varicose veins, flabby stomach, sagging breasts, constipation, haemorrhoids, urinary problems, prolapsed womb, back problems such as slipped disks, lack of self-esteem and depression – then practise your Yoga during pregnancy. Your chances of recovery are magnified manyfold. As an adjunct to this, do please get yourself checked by an osteopath or chiropractor after birth to prevent long-term damage and problems to your spine and pelvis.

The process of pregnancy is necessarily an engrossing, involving and absorbing one. However, this self-obsession can transmute into an ongoing obsession with one's offspring. I have seen too many women lose their interests, creative talents and even their personality whilst raising their children. They never seem to have a life of their own again. They invest their dreams and failures in their children. Instead of helping their growth, this can stifle the youngsters and stunt their development. Such obsessional preoccupation is not necessary. It is not a prerequisite for being a 'good mother', nor will it make you one. Yoga practice, particularly the self-observational routines, teach you the valuable lesson of your role in the birth process. As Kahlil Gibran so beautifully states: 'Your children are not your children. They are the sons and daughters of Life's longing for itself. They come through you but not from you, and though they are with you yet they belong not to you.'

Keeping up the practice

Although Yoga has been around for millennia, its practices and secrets were often the preserve of priestly castes and were simply unavailable for women. The sixties saw the first major exposition of this ancient science in the West and its recently revived popularity makes it accessible to all.

For novices, beginning Yoga offers the first opportunity to acquire life-long skills and regimes which meet far more than their immediate needs and provide a platform for future healthy living.

If you start your Yoga practice only during your pregnancy you have every excuse to keep up the habit. For some of my mothers it is the only time they have for themselves in the course of a busy week. Keeping up that discipline of weekly attendance is so easily lost and along with it precious friendships born of shared experience. As I have so often observed, there seems to be a special affinity between my Yoga students.

Yoga encapsulates the Eastern concept of 'less is more'. Its movement is dynamic so that you do not actually have to do a great deal. Once you have found your maximum comfortable stretch/position, mentally tune into the structure of the body and visualize it giving, stretching, easing and toning with very little effort and, more importantly, with no damage through repetition, strain or stress. This is the reason why more and more people are practising Yoga as opposed to other exercise systems – they instinctively know this is how the body really wants to move and work at its best.

If you are pregnant at this time, may I wish you good health and every happiness during your pregnancy, a safe and successful birth and a lifetime of joy with your offspring.

Guidelines for Best Practice

The following guidelines outline 'best practice'. Many of these preparations and preliminaries are universally accepted and even outlined in classical Yoga texts. To the basic and commonsense considerations, I have added elements that I have refined in my public classes and personal home practice. The reason I have drawn attention to them is to indicate the range of factors that I take into account when creating a sense of sacred space, both within the body and without. The successful combination of as many of these preliminaries as possible will make your practice not only more effective but hugely enjoyable and rewarding. As with all great work and art, the secret is in the preparation – you'll only get out of it what you put in.

Safety first

During pregnancy you are probably under the best medical scrutiny you will ever have experienced. The advice and monitoring given you by health professionals must be heeded at all times. I am pleased to say that Yoga has always been high on the recommended list of apt and appropriate regimes for pregnant women. With its accent on gentle stretching and working within the limitations of your body, it is perhaps the best health tool you could use at this special time. However, with all my students I undertake a health review, particularly in regard to the spine. If you have a history of prolapsed (slipped) disks or have suffered a whiplash injury or a fall, I recommend a visit to the osteopath or chiropractor before you engage in any Yoga practices. If you have any doubt about your condition, check with your health professionals and let them know what practices you are planning to use. If there is any show of blood you must stop immediately and seek medical advice.

Yoga classes

Although this book contains all the information you need to engage in healthy and safe Yoga practice, there is no substitute for personal tuition. Even so, it is important to find a teacher who is well-versed in the management of pregnancy and has the time and class size that allows for well-supervised sessions. The friendships and loving support that are part of such a class can last you a lifetime and offer valuable support long after your pregnancy. If you cannot find a qualified teacher or convenient class, why not consider inviting a few friends or other mothers-to-be to form a group and work from this book? The important thing is that the practices and sessions are regular and ongoing.

Preparing the environment

A number of key elements will ensure that your Yoga practice is a pleasant, enriching and rewarding experience. To achieve this, the creation of a sympathetic environment is crucial. The ideal place to practise is a pleasant, peaceful, sheltered, temperate, clean-aired, non-windy outdoor location. However, this is very rarely achievable and most people look to practise Yoga indoors where the environment can be better regulated.

When choosing your practice area, look for a special area that is not a thoroughfare for everyday activity. Ideally, for alignment purposes, it should allow you to face squarely onto a wall or view. The chosen area needs to be clean, free of clutter, as clear as possible and not too near a fire or furniture that could injure you if you fall or knock into it. It should be well-ventilated but not draughty, sweet-smelling, sympathetically lit and at a comfortable temperature. The floor must not be too hard, unless you practise on a non-slip rug or Yoga mat. Working in bare feet on a carpeted floor is ideal, although you should add an extra layer for comfort and support in the form of a folded blanket covered with a cotton sheet for seated or resting postures. There should be plenty of cushions or pillows to hand as you get larger and require more support.

Before you begin your Yoga practice, switch off any unnecessary electrical equipment, mute all telephones and divert calls to an answer facility. It's worth letting friends and family know the time of your regular practice so that they know not to contact you then, unless unavoidable. Some people enjoy the accompaniment of inspirational or atmospheric music, although a short period of real or relative silence, when you can tune into your breath and inner thoughts, is highly recommended.

Practice time

Yoga tradition suggests 4 am in the morning (*Brahmamuhurta*) as the ideal time for practice. Unless you are an insomniac or are having trouble sleeping, later in the morning should suffice! The morning is the best time for personal practice, although you will probably want to take part in a public class that would most likely take place in the evening. A combination of both morning and evening sessions will bring you the greatest benefits.

Cleansing

Before beginning, have a moderately hot shower to pre-warm your muscles and ligaments. A good scrub with a loofah or natural bristle brush will remove dead skin and invigorate your circulation. Moisturizing the skin with a nourishing lotion makes the skin more pliable. It also needs to be as fresh as possible – so that means no make-up!

Eating and drinking

Ideally, postures should be performed on an entirely empty stomach, so pre-breakfast would be the most obvious time to practise. I suggest starting the day with a small glass of warm, pre-boiled water to cleanse your system. If you suffer from low blood sugar you can suck a barley sugar sweet some time before practice. Empty your bladder and bowels before you start. Even if you suffer constipation, please avoid laxative drugs. Use Yoga and diet to address the condition (see page 68). Do not strain; just relax the body into the activity. If you choose the same time every day for your ablutions, after a few weeks your bowels will automatically need to evacuate at the same time every day. That's training for you!

Clothing and accessories

Consider the possibility of performing your Yoga nude and even observe yourself in a mirror if that's possible. This will enable you to align your posture more easily and observe, with fascination and wonderment, your ever-changing form. If you must wear clothes, ensure that they are loose-fitting, light, comfortable and preferably made from natural fabrics such as cotton and linen. Before practice, remove your glasses (or contact lenses, unless in a public class), wristwatch and jewellery.

Dynamic and static forms

All the practices in this book are suitable for any level of experience. Some of the more seasoned practitioners, however, may think these programmes are too easy. The key point is whether you utilize the postures in a dynamic or static way. Practised in a dynamic way they can be accomplished in a short time. They function almost as a dance form – one movement blending into another. This approach will increase flexibility, speed up circulation, loosen muscles and joints and release energy blocks.

Alternatively, the adoption of the postures can be slowed to a more static or meditative form. The static approach has a much more subtle and powerful effect on the energetic and mental bodies. If held for some minutes, with awareness, they will gently massage internal organs, glands and muscles and relax the nerves throughout the body. This approach is particularly beneficial for bringing the mind to a point of tranquillity and, eventually, to a state of sense withdrawal (*pratyahara*) – an essential prelude to higher states of concentration (*dharana*) and meditation (*dhyana*).

Energetic effects

In general, each group of postures gives a different energetic effect and can be categorized as follows:
• Standing postures give vitality.
• Sitting postures are calming.
• Twisting positions are cleansing.
• Inverted postures develop mental strength.
• Balancing brings a feeling of lightness.
• Backward bends are exhilarating.
• Forward bends have a refreshing effect on the brain.
• Lying prone (face downwards – definitely not for pregnant women!) is energizing.
• Lying supine (on the back) is restful.

Whichever posture you adopt, when it is perfectly aligned there will be no break in your energy flow.

Working methods

Yoga emphasizes the value of balance in all aspects of one's life. This is particularly true of your practice itself. Every bending posture should be followed by a counterstretch – a forward bend followed by a backward bend – and whatever you do to the left should be done to the right. I have carefully tailored the programmes to take account of this consideration and they include their own counterstretches in the form of winding down and relaxing conclusions.

If this is your first time practising Yoga or perhaps doing any significant exercise in some time, take the precaution of using the recommended warm-up routines from the antenatal series until you feel comfortable enough to start straight into a programme. Use the dynamic version of the postures at first, gradually lengthening your practice until you achieve and appreciate the benefits of the static form (as explained under Dynamic and Static Forms, see page 11).

There is an understandable tendency to practise any posture on a favoured side – the one that makes it easiest to accomplish. Get into the habit of first practising on the less comfortable side and give it the greatest attention. Over time the bias should become less obvious and the lack of poise or facility on one side will be addressed and corrected. No posture should ever be forced, held with strain or imposed with undue pressure, restriction or discomfort. Once you've found your maximum comfortable stretch, mentally tune into the structure of the body and visualize it giving, stretching, easing and toning while holding the posture. This static time is used to make subtle adjustments and alignments.

Breathing techniques

Control of the breath, or *pranayama*, is more than simply breathing, and basically consists of four stages. Primarily it consists of a conscious, prolonged inhalation embodying the act of receiving primal energy (*prana*). Retention is the savouring of that held breath. During exhalation,

thoughts and emotions are emptied with the outward flow of breath, and during external retention one surrenders that energy to its source.

I have included the more meditative and gentler of the classical techniques such as Sun and Moon Breathing (*Surya Bheda* and *Chandra Bhedana*), the Psychic Breath (*Ujjayi*) and the Psychic Network Purification (*Nadi Shodhana*), but do not recommend any of the more vigorous techniques or ones that involve prolonged retention of the breath or locks (*bhandas*). All the *pranayama* techniques are practised in a comfortable sitting position with the exception of the Complete Breath (see Yogic Breathing, pages 32–3) which is ideal in the standard relaxation posture (*Savasana*). The Birth Breaths, Feather Breathing and Candle Breathing (see pages 120–1), are specific to pregnancy but should be approached with the same concentration and awareness as the other *pranayamas*. Unless otherwise stated, all breathing should be through the nose rather than through the mouth.

No posture should be so strenuously or vigorously performed as to require great gulps of air or run the risk of hyperventilation. All postures should be synchronized with the rhythm of the breath, generally breathing in to extend, and out to contract. Even in the final position, do not hold the breath. Unless otherwise stated, breathe normally, taking one or two calming breaths between postures.

Deep relaxation

The best chance of deep relaxation will come after a thorough workout of the whole body with an integrated set of postures, followed by some *pranayamas*. Basically, the stronger the stretch the deeper the relaxation. I would recommend that every programme or session be followed by properly structured relaxation. Whether you choose a supine resting posture or a comfortable sitting position (see Postures for Seated Meditation, pages 90–1), spend a few minutes going through the techniques of Yogic Sleep (see *Yoga Nidra*, pages 20–1). Formulated by

Paramahansa Satyananda, one of the greatest living Yogis and Tantric Masters, and sourced from the ancient Tantric practice of *Nyasa*, it forms the basis of many modern-day adaptations. The key to it is a conscious and methodical relaxation of both body and mind.

Concentration and meditation

Relaxed concentration is the keystone of every Yoga practice. Whether you engage in the inwardly centring *Yoga Nidra* deep relaxation, or the concentrated gazing of the Candle Meditation (*Trataka*), fixed concentration is at the heart of it. It is a popular misconception that one can 'practise' meditation. Patanjali – codifier of the best-known classical Yoga treatise – reminds us that meditation is actually the consequence of continuous, unbroken concentration. You'll find that all the techniques outlined in this book have a strong element of visualization and this will help tremendously in your personal development as well as that of your unborn child.

Planning your Programme

Although I have arranged the various programmes into three sections, representing the three trimesters of pregnancy, you are not bound to practise only the ones for your stage. They are there as general safety guidelines to ensure that you do not over-extend yourself, particularly if you are coming to Yoga for the first time. If you have some Yoga experience, I am trusting to your best judgement the choice of how long to practise certain postures and at what point you make safe and appropriate adaptations to suit your changing condition.

In the last two trimesters I have put the accent on additional support, using extra pillows and chairs, and tailoring the posture work to a bodyform that is expanding to accommodate your baby and changing its balance and capabilities. Additionally, I have included postures that address the discomforts and conditions which women face during particular periods of their pregnancy, for example, lymphatic drainage techniques to help Carpal Tunnel Syndrome.

The Antenatal Programme (see pages 24–31) can be practised safely throughout pregnancy and may also be used as a warm-up to a schedule of practice using the various programmes outlined in each section. Since you may only have limited time for a session, I have crafted two 15-minute programmes for each trimester, giving the essence of a balanced practice. You can, however, 'mix and match' the various postures as long as you include the winding-down counterstretch that goes with it. If in doubt, remember that every forward bend should be accompanied by a backward bend and whatever you do to one side should be mirrored on the other.

If you have the time, do include a *pranayama* (breathing) technique after any posture session. It will both calm and settle the body, mentally and emotionally. The Complete Breath and The Psychic Breath (see Yogic Breathing, pages 32–3), and particularly the integrated practice of the Psychic Network Purification (see pages 92–3) are universally hailed for their safe and beneficial effects.

The ideal session would end with a destressing deep relaxation. I highly recommend that you use the *Yoga Nidra* sleep technique (see *Yoga Nidra*, pages 20–1), even in shortened form, to complete your practice.

Developing a balanced approach

I occasionally have to remind my students that they are neither in competition with each other nor themselves. In the West, due to concepts such as 'no pain, no gain', practitioners can have a tendency to strive too strongly to achieve perfection in their practice. The downside to trying to achieve goals is that it can lead to disincentivizing failure. There can be a tendency to sink into the past, using one's ailments as an excuse, or hanker for the future, grasping at the goal of a better body. The key is to stay in the moment, doing each step at a time to the best of your ability. You would not expect your baby to walk before it can crawl, so please treat your body with the same consideration. There is a fine line between discomfort and pain – it's called awareness.

The foundation of Yoga is balance. It is not primarily about how well you do your practice but what you learn about yourself as you are doing it. Please do not be discouraged if you seem stiff and ungainly. Yoga is not a race and you are not a hare. The long-term, gentle persistence of the tortoise will lead to injury-free practice, relaxed enjoyment, real self-knowledge and progress over time.

Although this book concentrates on the process of pregnancy, I do hope you will continue to use these Yoga practices right up until the miracle of your baby's birth and well into the future after the magical event.

Right: The book is divided into four sections (anticlockwise from top left: Antenatal, Early Pregnancy, Late Pregnancy and Mid-pregnancy), but don't feel that you have to adhere exclusively to those programmes designated for your stage.

The Chakras and Subtle Energies

'We use only one tenth of our brain.' How often have you heard that phrase? It has been said so often that most people take it for granted without having the slightest idea of what it implies. 'Perhaps Einstein or some great brain could do better,' they might say, 'but I seem to get along fine.'

Try the following exercise. Imagine spending your days and nights in a monochrome world lit, at best, with no more than feeble candlelight. What, then, would you make of a home lit with electric light and alive with colour? Would you be happy to go back to your old world and limited life once you had experienced that? Of course not. You would have discovered something better and would not be happy until you had possessed that dream home for yourself.

Take one further leap of the imagination ... What if you won millions on the Lottery and had free, uninterrupted and unlimited energy, your choice of any type of home you could imagine with any conceivable number and arrangement of rooms and an unlimited budget to furnish and decorate your home with the best of everything? Wouldn't that be your ultimate choice?

What, you might ask, has all this got to do with Yoga – those classes where people bend and stretch their bodies into strange shapes which are apparently good for your health? It is true that the postures look strange, but there's a great secret behind such odd behaviour. The ultimate purpose of practising Yoga is the awakening of *Kundalini Shakti*, the great evolutionary energy that is responsible for creating us as human beings in the first place.

Coiled like a serpent at the base of the spine (the perineum in man, the base of the cervix in woman), this potent and universal energy is the true maintainer of our body/mind. All Yoga practices, breathing techniques and meditations are geared towards one end – the arousal and distribution of this energy through a series of *chakras*, or energy centres, that are located along the spine.

A large number of people manage this trick only well enough to maintain reasonable health, a limited set of emotional responses, and thinking processes that get them by simply on a day-to-day basis – these are the monochrome home folk. In contrast, there are those people who choose health-giving foods, engage in and enjoy vitalizing exercise, have the sensitivity and courage to express a full range of emotions, including compassion and selflessness, and are able to visualize, plan and create. These are the vitalized home dwellers.

And then there are the rare and exceptional beings, the saints or spiritually super-rich who have given us the imperishable truths that inform all esoteric and religious systems. They are the spiritual teachers, sublime artists, the greatest scientists, healers, dancers and musicians whose wisdom and creations stir our souls beyond words and tears.

The power within

All this vast potential to enrich our lives is not hidden away in some inaccessible treasure-house or to be found in exotic faraway lands, but lies as close to us as our most intimate self. It is the very structure that supports our physical being. An energy blueprint or intricate network of subtle energies underlies our material body. These energies, known in the various esoteric and ancient medical systems as *prana*, *chi* or *ki*, flow along meridians or pathways called *nadis*. Traditionally 72,000 in number, three of them are considered to be the most important: *sushumna* that runs from tail to head, passing through each of the *chakras*; *ida*, the lunar or feminine channel; and *pingala*, the solar or masculine channel. *Ida* and *pingala* cross and interweave left and right from *chakra* to *chakra* and give us the age-old symbol for medicine, known as the *caduceus* or serpent-entwined winged staff of the messenger god Mercury. I still find it extremely odd that one of the greatest symbols of the esoteric and sacred energy system should be used by today's medical profession who do not even acknowledge its existence.

Tradition ascribes to the energy of each *chakra* a colour, a sound (*mantra*), and a visual form (*yantra*). Depending on the system you study, the books you read or the beliefs you hold, the exact number and position of these energy centres can vary. What is generally consistent is that the colours of the lower chakras start in the deep reds and move at a slower vibrational rate. As you move gradually upwards through the colour spectrum to violet and white, the frequency increases. The chakra energies are not religious in nature, although they are steeped in the Indian tradition that has done so much to keep the amazing science of Yoga alive today. And it *is* a science, and an empirical one at that. Known actions produce predictable results, time and time again.

As well as having a therapeutic physical effect, all Yoga postures have energetic ones related to the chakra system. A well-balanced programme will work on every level, releasing blocks and allowing a greater flow and intensity of energy from the infinite reservoir. Where appropriate, I will draw your attention to the particular centre that is most affected by the practice. As you become more attuned to the way your body functions through posture work, breathing, relaxation and meditation, you will become increasingly aware of the movement and flow of *Kundalini Shakti*. The noticeable effects are mostly subtle – a tingling sensation or a sense of warmth or coolness. The long-term benefits of greater vitality, postural poise, emotional balance, greater creativity and a compassionate nature will be there for all to see.

Below: *Kundalini Shakti* – our energy pathways.

sahasrara

ajna

vishuddhi

anahata

manipura

swadisthana

mooladhara

Deep Relaxation

Human beings were not designed for the twenty-first century. We have not evolved anything like fast enough to deal with the demands of a fast-paced, information-rich, stressful environment such as that which we find ourselves in today. In evolutionary terms we are still only in the Stone Age, perfectly adapted for life as a hunter-gatherer, not that of a business executive or a working mother.

Our endocrine system rules our life pretty effectively, releasing hormones – chemical messengers that regulate our metabolism, moods, sexuality and survival instincts. When the system is in proper balance we are positively oriented individuals with a healthy curiosity and zest for life. When, for any reason – physical, emotional or mental – that balance is disturbed or becomes irregular, or the system becomes overproductive, damaged or has simply been running on overdrive for far too long, then we are living stressed lives.

Modern life exposes us to a myriad of pressures, presenting problems that are often beyond our control. This produces a stress response from our endocrine system – a cocktail of hormones that prepares the body for physical or mental exertion. Unlike our ancestors with their short-term needs, we are required to keep our systems in overdrive just to cope sometimes. The long-term effect of this is a condition called chronic stress. Continued high levels of the stress hormone cortisol suppress the immune response, making us particularly vulnerable to viral infections, and can lead to heart attacks, cancer and memory loss. There are even recent findings that cortisol can find its way across the placenta affecting a baby's stress response in later life!

Stress in the twenty-first century is going to be one of the primary causes of health breakdowns. Unfortunately, there is no avoiding it: we all have to make choices on how we are going to deal with this problem. Coping skills ultimately fail us. Stepping onto the treadmill of life is all too easy – slowing down and switching off is another matter entirely.

Preparing to relax

Deep relaxation does not mean simply slumping in front of the television. It is a conscious activity which requires preparation, technique and regular practice. The key feature of all the many methods on offer, in the form of audio cassettes, CDs and books, is the reducing or switching off of signals generated by the senses.

As with preparations for an uninterrupted Yoga practice (see Guidelines for Best Practice, pages 10–11), creating the optimum environment is the first step. Adopting a comfortable and sustainable physical posture is the next. There are, of course, many options for this depending on your flexibility, how advanced your pregnancy is and how practised you are at relaxation techniques. Chair-sitting Westerners tend to have rather tight ligaments that make classical floor-seated postures such as the Lotus (*Padmasana*) and its variants hard to achieve or maintain. Sitting in a chair that supports the back well and keeps the posture in reasonable alignment is one option. The other is to adopt a supine (lying on your back) position where gravity can assist the process. The classic Corpse Posture, known as *Savasana* (see page 20), or one like the illustration opposite which is comfortably supported and adapted for your pregnant body, is ideal.

Releasing the mind

Having physically reduced sensory information by closing your eyes, reducing light to non-distracting levels, keeping audio stimuli to a minimum or using it as background sound and relieving the body's tensions by easing movements, you can move on to desensitizing the mind to distracting stimuli. The practice of *Yoga Nidra* (outlined on pages 20–1) is a fine example of a progressively body-quietening method.

At this point one of two things happens. Either you fall asleep because your body has been given the usual cues to close down or – more rarely – your consciousness is freed from total identification with the body, and you achieve that detached state that is sometimes experienced between waking and sleeping. You are aware that you are an entity but as a consciousness that exists without reference to bodily identification. This is the first stage of a state called *Pratyahara* – sense withdrawal – and is the indispensable first step towards the higher Yogic practices.

Typically at this time your mind will be flooded with thoughts, which might seem a little alarming if this is your first experience of opening yourself up to this level of awareness. But don't be concerned; the clearing process that goes on in the brain is similar to that experienced during REM (rapid eye movement) sleep. It is a necessary function of the brain and therefore quite natural. The difference is that you are conscious and aware of the process. You are likely to perceive what you think of as 'good' and 'bad' thoughts and a whole range of images thrown up by the subconscious mind. Do not be frightened or drawn into them. Just imagine that you are watching a movie being displayed on the screen behind your closed eyes (*Chidakasha* – the 'Space of Consciousness'). Don't be tempted to get drawn into attractive thoughts (happy memories, fantasies, etc.) or try to suppress unpleasant thoughts (negative views of yourself, feelings of anger, etc.) – 'treat those two imposters just the same', and become an observer instead. In time,

if you continue to work with visualization or concentration techniques, the flood of thoughts will subside to a steady trickle and eventually be no more than occasional visitors.

Mind power

Deep relaxation offers you yet another potential reward. The time you spend in this fluid physical, emotional and mental state is the ideal time to plant positive affirmations that you would like to implement in your life. The power of suggestion can neutralize destructive habits and plant seeds that bear fruit without effort. The short, positively worded resolution (*Sankalpa*) is a statement of intent. Choose a realizable short-term goal, perhaps relating to the health of you and your baby. On a physical level it might be something like: 'I resolve to take regular exercise' or 'I resolve to quit smoking'. On a more spiritual plane it might be: 'I will become more aware' or 'I will be kindlier to all beings'. Practised regularly during your deep relaxation periods, such resolutions can transform your life.

Below: A comfortable lying posture adapted for the pregnant body.

Practising Yoga Nidra

The following deep-relaxation practice of *Yoga Nidra* (Yogic Sleep) was formulated by Paramahansa Satyananda based on the little known, but very important, Tantric practice of *Nyasa*. This systematic rotation of consciousness can induce complete physical, mental and emotional relaxation. Ordinarily, when you lay down to sleep and dissociate yourself from sensory input, the inclination is to fall asleep. This practice, calling for special concentration and awareness, can help you to experience that space between sleep and wakefulness. This is where contact with the subconscious or unconscious dimensions of the mind can be made.

You may care to record the following section on a cassette tape to enable you to establish the pattern until the sequence can be remembered and mentally repeated. Alternatively, ask a friend to guide you through the practice until you are familiar with it. Don't change the routine once that pattern has been set in your mind. Remember, the object is to stay awake and aware throughout the practice. Do not be discouraged if you fall asleep the first few times: persevere until you can regularly achieve this state.

Lie on your back in *Savasana*, the Corpse Posture, illustrated opposite. Rest your arms freely by your sides, palms uppermost, arms straight but not rigid, in a natural diagonal line away from your body. Relax your fingers and let them curl naturally into the palms. Make sure your head is in alignment with your feet, your legs slightly parted and falling open from the hips. Gently close your eyes and keep them closed. Your breathing should be natural and through your nose. There should be no physical movement during the practice. Become aware of your whole body from head to toe and be completely still.

Starting at the right thumb, mentally repeat the name of each part of the body in the sequence outlined. As you name each body part, simultaneously become aware of it, mentally releasing and relaxing. Pause for a second or two between each mention of a body part to allow mental repetition. Take your time.

'Right-hand thumb (pause) ... second finger (pause) ... third finger ... fourth finger ... little finger ... palm of the hand ... back of the hand ... wrist ... forearm ... elbow ... upper arm ... shoulder... armpit ... side of the body... hip ... thigh ... knee ... back of the knee ... shin ... calf ... ankle ... heel ... sole ... instep ... big toe ... second toe ... third toe ... fourth toe ... little toe.'

Repeat the sequence starting with the left-hand thumb. Now focus your attention on the back. Become aware of:

'the right shoulder blade ... the left shoulder blade ... the right buttock ... the left buttock ... the spine ... the whole back together.'

Now focus your attention on:

'the top of the head ... the forehead ... both sides of the head ... the right eyebrow ... the left eyebrow ... the space between the eyebrows ... the right eyelid ... the left eyelid ... the right eye ... the left eye ... the right ear ... the left ear ... the right cheek ... the left cheek ... the chin ... the throat ... the right side of the chest ... the left side of the chest ... the middle of the chest ... the navel ... the abdomen.'

Now focus your attention on:

'the whole of the right leg ... the whole of the left leg ... both legs together ... the whole of the right arm ... the whole of the left arm ... both arms together ... the whole of the back ...the buttocks ... the spine ... the shoulder blades ... the whole of the front ... the abdomen ... the chest ... the whole of the back and the front ... the whole of the head ... the whole body together ... the whole body ... the whole body.'

At this point, and far more quickly after regular practice, you should be largely free of distracting sensory input. By far the simplest, though nonetheless effective, concentration practice one can do at this moment is to observe one's natural breathing. Visualization of a personal sacred symbol and repetition of one's *Sankalpa* (see Mind Power, page 19) are further extensions you can utilize. When you have completed your practice, gently stir your fingers, hands, etc., and bring your awareness back to your physical body.
Yoga Nidra is complete.

Posture, Poise and Balance

To be able to really enjoy the therapeutic benefits of Yoga, you need to learn how to recondition your body through postural alignment and fine-tuning – in other words, to discover ways to adjust the basic structure and use an internal reference for everyday movements. Although it might seem a little laborious to observe all of the following precautions, learning the proper procedures for sitting, rising and standing will preserve your joints and also tone your muscles. Being conscious of the way you sit, stand, walk and rest can remove fatigue, refresh the brain, soothe the nerves and help to regulate blood pressure. Proper alignment of the body can ease and prevent indigestion, heartburn and breathing difficulties.

Sitting correctly

When they sit down, too many people, whether pregnant or not, collapse like a sack of potatoes into their chairs. The fact that this is so inelegant shows that it is an abuse of posture and a strain on the joints. Holding yourself well and not allowing your weight to sink into the joints, whether sitting or standing, will prevent undue pressure on you and your baby.

1

2

3

4

[1] Seated posture

Sit with your base vertebrae against the back of a chair, legs comfortably apart. Keep your feet flat on the floor if possible, resting on a book(s) if necessary. Lean slightly forwards from the base to allow deeper breathing in the lower part of your lungs. 'Grow up' through the spine, creating space between your thighs and trunk. » Tilt the front of your pubic bone slightly forwards to align the pelvis and to sit on the anus. Balance your head above the base of the spine, arms hanging freely, hands resting lightly in your lap with the fingers loose and not interlaced. Breathe naturally, expanding your chest and ribcage muscles.

[2] Preparing to rise

Ease to the edge of your seat, raise your left heel, resting on the ball of the foot. Rest your hands on your thighs to help stabilize the movement. Imagine you are balancing a book on your head.

[3] Rising without strain

Push up with the power of your left foot and thighs. Keep the weight evenly distributed on both feet. Allow your arms to hang freely by your sides.

[4] Sitting without strain

To reverse the procedure, stand close to the chair with your left heel raised, resting on the ball of the foot and with the back of your legs against the chair. Slowly lower your body using the power of your thighs and keeping an upright carriage.

Standing correctly – Mountain Posture

What may seem like the simplest act – that of standing straight and still – is actually one of the most difficult to accomplish and maintain. Performed correctly, *Tadasana*, or Mountain Posture, with its precise placements, correct extensions and alignments, encapsulates all the principles and possibilities inherent in every Yoga posture. It is one of the best gauges of progress.

[1] Stand facing squarely onto a wall or a full-length mirror if you have one. Place your feet together, toes in line with the heels. If possible, have both the outer edges of your big toes and their ball joints touching, as well as your ankle bones. Keep your weight evenly distributed on the inner and outer edges of your feet, ensuring that the arches are lifted as your body adjusts. Be light on your feet.

[2] Lift your weight off the ankles, Achilles' tendons, knees and hips. Lengthen your spine through to the skull as the upward flow pulls back the knees, opens the diaphragm and expands the chest as you pull the shoulders backwards and also downwards.

[3] Let your arms hang freely and slightly away from your torso, allowing them to rotate slightly to present the biceps muscles and elbow creases to the fore whilst the palms face into the body.

[4] Tuck in your buttocks and contract the anus to push the coccyx (base of the spine) and sacrum (centre of the pelvis) forwards and upwards.

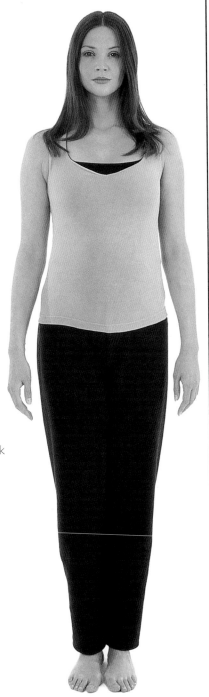

To fine-tune the movement, extend the whole of the back of your neck from a point between your shoulder blades, ensuring that your chin is at right angles to your chest and the top of your ears are immediately above the lobes. Release your facial mask and expressions, relax your jaw and look forwards with a soft focus. Breathe naturally as you visualize your body being as steady as a mountain.

Stretching and toning exercises

The following set of antenatal exercises (pages 24–33) are extremely safe, easy to perform and effective. Encompassing standing, sitting and floor work, they stretch and tone the whole body in a slow and rhythmical pattern. They are suitable for all stages of pregnancy and may be utilized either in a dynamic manner as a warm-up session to later programmes, or in their static and more meditative form as a complete session in themselves.

[1] Clenching and opening the fists

Start by checking your posture in the classical *Tadasana* (see Standing correctly, page 23). Adopt your starting position by turning your toes out for secure balance. Exhale, then inhale as you raise your arms, in elegant ballet style, forwards and upwards into a 'V' shape, palms facing each other. Keep a sense of spaciousness in your chest and ribcage and do not hunch or tighten your shoulders. Swivel your wrists to face the front and exhale as you firmly clench them (see 1A). Your awareness should remain on your whole body form, not just on your hands.

» With your next natural inhalation, unclench your fists and fully extend your fingers (see 1B). Again, when you are ready to exhale, clench your fists.

» Repeat the clenching and unclenching movements three times (or more if you feel comfortable). When the sequence is completed, inhale as you turn your palms to face one another. Exhale as you gracefully lower your arms to just below shoulder level, turning the palms downwards before returning to your starting position.

» Take one or two natural breaths before you continue with the next step.

1A   1B

[2] Circling the elbows

Exhale. Inhale as you raise your hands, elbows to the side, and lightly touch your fingers onto your shoulders. Exhale as you circle your elbows downwards and forwards, touching briefly. Keep the movement fluid as you begin the upward circle, inhaling to expand your chest and ribcage and taking your elbows backwards and around to the starting position. **»** Exhale as the elbows move forwards to touch and inhale as they circle upwards into the next circle. **»** Maintaining this breathing pattern and circling to the maximum extent, slowly and consciously complete at least six to ten full circles. Return to your starting position and breathe naturally.

2

[3] Circling the hips

Stand with your feet comfortably apart. Breathing naturally throughout, bend your knees, simultaneously pushing your hips to the right and echoing the movement with the heels of your hands (see 3A). **»** Rest your hands on your pelvis and rotate your hips backwards and around to the left (see 3B), again echoing the movement with your hands, with the fingers pointing in the opposite direction to the flow of the movement. Rest them back on the pelvis as you circle forwards to complete the first sequence. **»** Circle three times clockwise then three times anticlockwise. This sequence loosens the hips and pelvis.

3A   3B

[4] Standing pelvic tilt

Stand with your feet slightly apart, hands cradling your hip bones. Bend your knees as you lean your torso slightly forwards (see 4A). Inhale as you slide your hands around to support your buttocks. » Exhale as you contract your pelvis, tucking your buttocks, coccyx (base of the spine) and sacrum (centre of the pelvis) inwards and upwards (see 4B). Hold for a few seconds, feeling the stretch, before inhaling and returning to the starting position. Repeat six times. » Stand with your feet hip-width apart and repeat the sequence a further six times.

[5] Pliés

Pliés are a ballet movement. The sequence will work well on the inner thighs and hips as well as imparting poise, grace and balance. It can be performed holding onto a sink, table or chair back. Start with your heels touching, toes turned out, and your hands resting on the support (see 5A). » Inhale, then exhale as you bend at the knees and descend slowly into a diamond shape (see 5B). Keep your spine in alignment and make sure you do not 'ducktail' your hips and stick out your bottom. Inhale as you straighten up. Slowly repeat the sequence six times, synchronizing your breathing. » Step your feet comfortably astride, turning your toes out a little further than before. As you bend, move your knees outwards to a point over the little toes (see 5C). » Repeat the sequence a further six times.

4A

4B

5A

5B

5C

[6] Sitting pelvic tilt

Sit towards the front of a chair with your feet comfortably apart and your hands resting on your upper thighs (see 6A). Inhale, then exhale as you lean back into your pelvis, tucking in your buttocks, coccyx and sacrum to draw up the pelvic floor. Your chin should naturally relax towards your chest, but not rest on it (see 6B).
» Inhale, and return to the starting position. Repeat the sequence six times. » Then place your palms over your hip bones. Inhale, drawing up your pelvic floor as if it is a lift you are drawing up to the first floor of an imaginary building (see 6C). Then exhale as you slowly relax it down to the cellar. Repeat slowly six times, with awareness.

6A

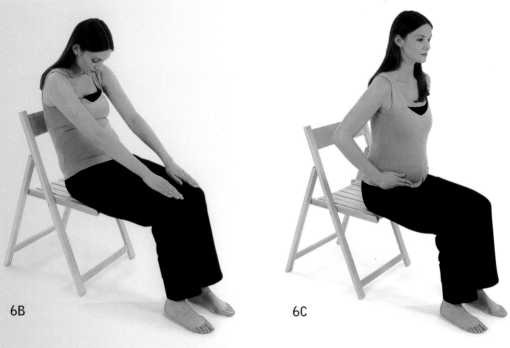

6B

6C

7A

7B

7C

7D

[7] Kneeling pelvic tilt

In addition to toning the pelvis and upper arms, this sequence gives the neck and shoulder region a destressing stretch.

» Kneel on all fours with your knees in a vertical line from the hips and hip-width apart, your arms shoulder-width apart and vertical from the shoulders. Your elbows should be contracted so that the top of the biceps (the upper-arm muscles) and elbow creases are facing forwards. Your palms should be flat on the floor with your head in line with the base of your spine (see 7A).

» Inhale, then exhale as you tuck your pelvis inwards and upwards, curving your spine like an awakening cat (see 7B). Tuck your head inwards, with your chin towards your chest. » At this point you can gain an increased benefit by rising up onto your fingertips (see 7C). Release the fingertip stretch, and inhale as you return to the starting position. Repeat the sequence six times, in emulation of the lithesome cat.

» From the starting position, inhale once again. Exhale as you walk your hands around to the right side of your body, towards your feet (see 7D). When you have reached your maximum comfortable stretch, inhale and walk your hands back to the starting position. Walk your hands around to the left side as a counterbalance, repeating the whole sequence five further times to each side.

[8] Paddling and circling the feet

This sequence works strongly on toning and stretching the leg muscles as well as easing tensions in the ankles, knees and hips. It is particularly effective in dealing with swollen ankles. **»** Sit in an upright position on the floor, extending your arms behind you and using them to prop up your body. Breathing naturally throughout, arch and flex your feet alternatively (see 8A). One foot should extend with a maximum stretch towards the floor, whilst the other flexes back towards you, even lifting slightly off the floor if possible. Repeat at least ten times, more if you wish. **»** From the same starting position, open your legs approximately hip-width apart. Breathing naturally, circle your feet outwards and away from each other in wide circles (see 8B). Take your time and bring your full awareness to the task. Repeat ten times. **»** Reverse the direction to circle your feet inwards towards each other (see 8C). Again, repeat ten times with full awareness. **»** Finally, with the heels together, circle both feet in a clockwise direction ten times, then reverse and circle anticlockwise ten times (see 8D).

8A

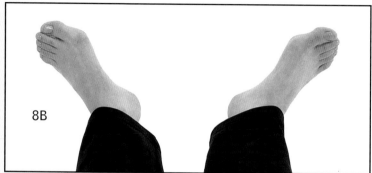

8B

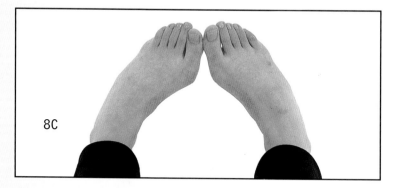

8C

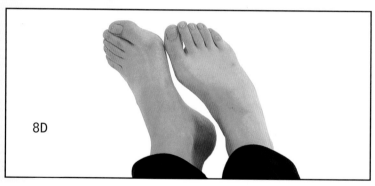

8D

[9] Butterflies

Most chair-sitting Westerners have short and tight ligaments which prevent the knees unfolding easily to the floor. The butterfly exercises not only prepare the ligaments for birth delivery but are an essential prerequisite to the classical sitting postures such as the Lotus Position (*Padmasana*). **»** Sit in an upright position on the floor, propping up your body with your arms extended behind you, and forming a loose diamond shape with your bent knees (see 9A). **»** Lean gently forwards and lace your fingers around your toes and the outer edges of your feet, pressing the soles together. Pull your feet as close into your pelvic girdle as possible, whilst still maintaining an upright spine (see 9B). Breathing naturally, flap your knees up and down like a butterfly's wings. Be aware of the gentle and progressive stretch given to the ligaments at the top of the inner thighs. Continue for about half a minute, ensuring that the soles of the feet remain together. **»** To strengthen the ligament stretch once you have warmed up, inhale then exhale as you press the knees outwards and downwards with your elbows (see 9C). Hold momentarily and, inhaling, return to the upright position. Repeat the butterfly movements for another half minute or so, then repeat the pressing movement.

9A

9B   9C

[10] Lying pelvic tilt: arching and extending

Lie on the floor with your head supported by a cushion or folded towel, your knees bent and your legs comfortably apart and in line with your hips. Your arms should be free from the sides of your body, palms down. **»** Exhale, then inhale, arching the small of your back and ribcage and tilting your pelvis upwards. Exhale, slowly contracting your pelvic floor and pressing and extending your back into and along the ground. Hold momentarily and repeat six times.

10

Yogic Breathing

Air contains not only oxygen but also the universal life force and energy (*prana*, *chi* or *ki*). We receive air through our lungs and blood supply into every body cell and yet, generally, we breathe superficially, using a mere one sixth of our lung capacity. We usually leave everyday breathing to haphazard control by the body's automatic reflexes and the unconscious mind. Yogic breathing aims to bring the whole breathing cycle under conscious control. We do it by becoming aware of the body mechanisms involved and deliberately modifying the rhythm and force of our breathing.

The simplest of the Yogic breathing exercises is The Complete Breath, not to be confused with deep breathing. A Complete Breath involves all the stale air being expelled from the lungs before fresh air is drawn in, and the whole of your torso being free to participate in the process. Far too many people suffer from a form of 'frozen torso', trying to breathe without moving the ribs and, worse still, bloating the abdomen.

Practising the following steps will familiarize you with all the stages of The Complete Breath. When you are comfortable and familiar with the individual techniques, practise them together. Keep your practice subtle. Simply imagine you are breathing in the scent of a beautiful flower.

The Complete Breath will help you to gain control of your breath, correct poor breathing habits and increase your oxygen intake, ensuring a rich blood supply for your baby. It may be practised at any time, but will be especially useful in calming the nerves during situations of high stress or anger. Used regularly, it will help to regulate mood swings.

There are many useful and beautiful images one can add to this practice to make it even more effective. For example, the relationship between the mind and the breath may be likened to a mother who cherishes her child with loving care or, more powerfully, as a turbulent river which, when harnessed by dams and canals, will provide abundant energy. One of my 'Yoga mothers' used the following imagery with great effect during her delivery. While breathing in she imagined that the in-breath was a painkiller, and when she breathed out she let go all of her pain and discomfort. For the purposes of this practice it is appropriate to know the definitions and locations of the regions referred to as abdominal, thoracic and clavicular. The abdominal area is the lower part of the trunk below the stomach and including the large intestine, centred around the navel. The thoracic area refers to the middle lobes of the lungs encompassed by the ribcage. The clavicular area contains the upper ribs and the area around the collar bone.

Breathing practice

[1] Abdominal breathing

Sit on a meditation stool or a rolled or folded blanket, ensuring that your spine is in a straight line, but not ramrod straight. Lean very slightly forwards from the base of the spine. As a guide if you are a novice, place your hands on your abdomen just above the navel, with your middle fingertips touching, so that you can feel your abdomen expand and contract. Exhale, then gently inhale, drawing air into the lower lobes of the lungs and allowing your abdomen to expand gently, forcing your fingertips apart. Your ribcage and chest should not expand during this breath. Exhale slowly as the diaphragm moves upwards, the abdomen moves downwards and the fingertips touch again. Repeat six times. If you wish, make the sound 'Ah' (as in 'arm') as you exhale.

1

[2] Thoracic breathing

Place your hands on either side of your ribcage, your fingertips touching, and inhale without using your diaphragm or expanding your abdomen. Feel your ribs moving outwards and upwards, drawing air into your lungs. Exhale by relaxing your chest muscles and feel the air being expelled from your lungs. Repeat six times. If you wish, make the sound 'Oh' (as in 'throw') as you exhale.

[3] Clavicular breathing

Place your hands on the upper part of your chest by the clavicles. Inhale using the thoracic breathing technique. When your lungs are fully expanded, inhale a little more, feeling your shoulders and collarbones move up slightly. Exhale slowly, releasing the air from your ribcage and finally expelling it from the upper chest. If you wish, make the sound 'Mm' (as in 'hum') as you exhale.

2

3

The Complete Breath

This technique is a combination of the abdominal, thoracic and clavicular breathing sequences. You do not need to place your hands in position on the torso since you have already demonstrated to yourself the previous processes. Do not strain or make undue noise when practising this technique: let your breath be smooth and gentle, like the swelling of the sea.

Sitting with your hands relaxed in your lap or in a gesture such as *Chin Mudra* (hand gesture illustrated right), inhale slowly and deeply, utilizing your diaphragm and allowing your abdomen to expand. As you reach the end of the abdominal expansion and without pause or notable transition, start to expand your ribcage outwards and upwards. When your ribs are fully expanded, continue the inhalation until the clavicular area is filled.
» Exhale, allowing the diaphragm to push upwards and the abdomen to contract, then emptying the ribcage and finally expelling the air from the clavicular area. This is one complete breath. Repeat ten times. If you wish, as you exhale you can make the sound 'Aum' ('ah-oh-mm') – which is the nearest vocal equivalent of the sublime sound said to represent the cosmic ground of being.

The Psychic Breath

One of the classic *pranayamas*, and suitable for every practitioner and in any position, *Ujjayi* has a healing effect on the body, a soothing effect on the nervous system and a tranquillizing effect on the mind. It can help relieve insomnia and, since it slows down the heart-rate, helps those suffering from high blood pressure.

Imagine that your breath is being drawn in and out, not through the nostrils but through the throat. As your breathing deepens, gently contract the glottis (opening of the larynx or windpipe) so that you can quietly hear a soft snoring sound like the breathing of a sleeping baby. *Ujjayi* can be practised for several minutes at a time, either on its own or in conjunction with The Complete Breath.

Early Pregnancy

The First Trimester

up to 14 weeks

Baby's arms and legs are starting to form and the face is beginning to develop its own unique appearance.

The reproductive organs are developed but it is difficult to distinguish the gender.

At 12 weeks, your baby is about the size of an avocado pear.

Baby's heart is beating and blood is flowing around the body.

Baby is able to suck, swallow and urinate.

Baby is 6–8 cm (2½–3 inches) long and weighs 12 g (½ oz).

Everyplace the Great Spirit dwells
Is the source of a gentle crystalline light

And within that light we become one
Floating as if in our mother's warm body
Living together as children of the earth

Without time
Without end ...

Kitaro

Natural Home Health Help

In the first trimester of pregnancy (up to 14 weeks) you might well expect to experience one or more of the following changes or conditions. Their severity or debilitating effect will depend greatly on the state of preparedness of your physical body and also your emotional and mental state.

There is no need to be alarmed at these changes. Regular Yoga practice will address and alleviate most of them so that they become either negligible or merely part of your development at this stage of pregnancy. Other natural health and commonsense remedies, culled from a range of both ancient and modern sources, can also prove to be beneficial.

Morning sickness

The term 'morning sickness' is pretty much a misnomer for anyone who has realized that it is not only during the morning that this particular affliction can strike. Unfortunately for some, sickness can occur throughout the whole pregnancy, although this is extremely rare. The condition is caused by hormonal changes and usually settles down once the placenta has taken over hormone production at around 12 to 14 weeks. To prevent it – or at least to reduce its intensity – try the following:

- Sip either hot or cold water first thing in the morning to alleviate the symptoms of morning sickness.

- If you do eat eggs, make sure that you check them for freshness and cook them well.

- Drink pure mineral waters and ginger, peppermint or camomile teas.

- Eat fresh fruit such as pears, peaches, nectarines, ripe bananas and seedless grapes, and add fresh ginger to stir-fries.

- Since the secret of keeping your blood sugar at appropriate levels is to eat little and often, you can freely treat yourself to biscuits made from bran, arrowroot or oats.

- Avoid 'diet' or sweet fizzy drinks, saccharine, rich cheeses, liver or foods that are chemically treated, highly spiced, fatty or acidic.

- Absolutely avoid alcohol and smoking or smoky environments, particularly during the early stages of pregnancy. The dangers of both should, by now, be more than obvious.

- Wear travel sickness bands – this can be quite effective. Do *not* be tempted to take travel sickness tablets.

- Learn the shiatsu and acupressure points to help alleviate the symptoms.

Digestive upsets

There are several practical steps you can take to prevent digestive upsets:

- Sit right up to the table and support your back at mealtimes to avoid unnecessary pressure on the digestive tract.

- Chew your food slowly and carefully and give yourself more time for it to be digested before you start moving around.

- Don't drink and eat at the same time: drink 10 minutes before eating or 15 minutes afterwards.

- Eat proteins and carbohydrates separately as this makes it easier for the body to digest them

- Prop yourself up in bed at night, using a 'V'-shaped pillow to prevent indigestion or heartburn.

Urinary problems

You may find that you feel the need to urinate more than usual. This is perfectly normal in the first few months and the latter part of the pregnancy, and is due to an increase in waste fluids and the improved efficiency of the kidneys. Of course, there is also increased pressure on the bladder from the growing baby.

• When you urinate, lean forwards to ensure that you empty the bladder completely.

• Limit your fluid intake after 4 pm if you want an uninterrupted night's sleep.

• Do not limit your fluid intake during the day, although it is advisable to cut down on tea and coffee because these can act as diuretics (agents that encourage the discharge of urine), which can aggravate the problem.

Fatigue

The body needs time to adjust to the miraculous changes taking place within it, resulting in feelings of fatigue. Keeping an eye on your daily routines and making some adjustments of your own means you need not suffer in silence.

• Start practising the art of relaxation and give yourself a little longer to accomplish everyday chores.

• If you find it difficult to sleep at night, practise your relaxation techniques and find time to rest during the day – even 20 minutes will be beneficial.

• Get some fresh air every day with a brisk walk if possible, which will also do wonders for toning your pelvic floor.

• Don't allow your blood sugar to drop – regulate it by eating little and often. Healthy suggestions include: a banana and yogurt blended with wheatbran and honey, or freshly made porridge with honey or maple syrup. Both of these will add fuel to your boiler and get the metabolism going.

• Energy levels can drop without warning, so no skipped meals!

Tender breasts

One of the very earliest signs of pregnancy is tender or tingling breasts. If this becomes a problem for you, try these remedies:

• Apply hot or cold flannels or even a packet of cold peas to the breasts.

• Massage your breasts gently. This can bring a measure of relief as well as being an excellent toning preparation.

• Avoid caffeine in the form of tea and coffee.

• In preparation for breast-feeding, avoid using soap on your nipples as this can be drying.

Pelvic Poses

This introductory sequence is an ideal start to your programme. The Pelvic Tilt and Pelvic Clock give you time to adjust your body in a comfortable position and are a follow-up to the earlier antenatal pelvic floor exercises. The Pelvic Clock is an excellent movement to use as part of a postnatal 'recovery' exercise regime. You can use the unique massage and movement approach to bring yourself back into shape.

Benefits from this sequence include increased pelvic flexibility and relief from lumbar backache. It is also an excellent diuretic because it drains the legs, helping to prevent varicose veins. The abdominal massaging eases constipation and piles and relieves pressure on the hip joints, knees and ankles. The Pelvic Tilt and Clock can be performed throughout pregnancy, although you must ensure proper support with additional cushions under your head and shoulders.

Concentrations and mental awareness of a chakra or psychic energy node greatly improves the understanding and effectiveness of every posture. For this sequence your energetic focus is on the basal chakras, *mooladhara* and *swadhistana* (see page 17).

Your imaginative thought might be:
'There is more to life than the measuring of speed and time.'

1

[1] The Pelvic Tilt

Take up a starting position lying on the floor with your head supported by a cushion, or your neck by a small rolled hand towel. For comfort, keep your hair away from the back of your neck. **»** Rest your legs on a chair seat and, if your feet are lower than your knees, rest them on a cushion. Settle down until your mind and body become quiet and still. **»** Relax your facial expression and rest in this version of *Savasana*, the Corpse Posture, for two to three natural breaths. **»** Exhale, then inhale for a count of five (mentally count 'one and two and three and four and five'), while arching your lower back, expanding your chest and tilting your pelvis. **»** Exhaling for a count of five, pull your lower back gently into the floor and your pelvic floor inwards and upwards. Repeat the step six times.

[2] The Pelvic Clock

In your starting position, rest your hands on your hips. Maintaining a natural pattern of breathing, form a loose diamond shape with your legs by placing the soles of your feet together. **»** Think of your lower back as the face of a clock. Press your navel into the floor (12 o'clock), and, while still lying flat on your back, press and accentuate the pressure onto the back of your left hip (3 o'clock). **»** Continuing in the same slow, circling action, bring pressure to bear onto your coccyx or tailbone (6 o'clock), then over to the right (9 o'clock) and back up to the navel again (12 o'clock). **»** Roll around the circumference of the lower back to massage the muscles and roll the pelvis. Repeat six times clockwise and six times anticlockwise. Rest for a few natural breaths back in the starting position.

2

The Bridge

Based on the classical *Setu Bandhasana*, The Bridge, this back bend resembles the span of a bridge. As you arch your back, your spine lengthens in one long, smooth curve, symbolizing the spirit of man bridging time and eternity.

The benefits of The Bridge include the stretching and strengthening of the abdominal and back muscles, which helps to develop a supple back and strong wrists. The pressure, when applied to the back of the ribs, is an excellent diuretic as it stimulates the kidneys. The controlled chin lock (*bandha*) slightly pressurizes the blood flow to the thyroid region and, once released in the winding-down position, the refreshed and increased blood flow cleanses and flushes out the gland, helping to activate the metabolism.

Your energetic focus is on the navel area, *manipura chakra* (see page 17). Your imaginative thought might be: **'I am a flexible connection.'**

Safety note
Do not practise The Bridge if you suffer from high blood pressure, heart disease or stomach ulcers.

1

2

[1] Lie flat on your back with your knees bent and feet in line with your hips. Exhale, then inhale for a count of five as you raise your trunk and arch your body.

[2] Exhale, interlacing your fingers. Inhale and ease up onto your shoulders as you straighten your arms to form a firm triangular base, contracting your shoulder blades and expanding your chest. **»** Contract your buttocks and push your hips upwards to strengthen the back. Hold for about two to three natural breaths.

[3] Inhale and rise onto the balls of your feet. **»** Exhale, pressing your hands into your hips, small of the back or ribcage (fingers turned inwards) for support. **»** Hold this static stretch for two to three natural breaths, easing yourself into your maximum comfortable position.

[4] If your position feels well balanced, raise your right foot onto your left thigh. **»** Hold and balance for two to three natural breaths. **»** Now relax your right leg and bring your left foot onto your right thigh, still breathing naturally.

3

[5] Winding down

Now wind down. Slowly lower your raised leg. Release your arms from the supporting position and press them into the floor to provide leverage. **»** Lower your heels and simultaneously press the muscles of your shoulders, back and hips into the floor. **»** This gives a strong massage as the body comes into a supine position. Relax into the resting position of *Savasana*, breathing in your natural rhythm and experiencing a sense of uplift.

4

5

The Fish

According to Hindu mythology, *Matsya*, the fish, was one of the incarnations of the god Vishnu, who took this form in order to save the world from the Flood. The Fish, *Matsyasana*, is a counterpose to The Bridge (see pages 40–1), *Setu Bandhasana*. You should stay in the pose at least half the time you held The Bridge to help complement and balance the previous stretch.

Benefits include relief for all kinds of abdominal ailments including inflamed and bleeding piles. The arched and expanded posture helps asthma and bronchitis by encouraging deeper respiration. Stagnant blood is recirculated from the back and can alleviate backache. *Matsyasana* regulates the functioning of the thyroid gland and stimulates the thymus, giving a boost to the immune system. It is particularly beneficial in helping to combat depression and mood swings and restores a sense of youthfulness and vitality.

Your energetic focus is on *manipura* or *anahata chakra* (see page 17). Your imaginative thought might be: **'I am floating in an ocean of bliss.'**

Safety note
Do not practise The Fish if you suffer from heart disease, peptic ulcers, a hernia or a serious back condition such as whiplash.

[1] Start with your knees bent and your arms by your side close to the body, palms facing downwards. Use a rolled towel or firm cushion beneath you for support, if necessary.

1

[2] Exhale, then inhale and arch onto the crown of your head using the power of your back muscles and the support of your forearms. Think of your ribcage as the gills of a fish in order to open and expand your lung capacity. Open your knees into a diamond shape, with the soles of the feet touching and your hips opening. Hold for about two to three natural breaths.

[3] Bring your knees up, legs slightly apart, and hold the position for two to three natural breaths.

[4] Maintaining a natural breathing pattern, raise your right leg and hold for two to three breaths. Lower the leg and repeat with the left leg.

[5] Now wind down by resting in the starting position, removing the supporting cushion to allow your back to rest flat on the floor. You may wish to place the rolled towel under your knees to relieve the pressure on the small of the back. Breathe naturally.

2

3

4

5

The Crossover Twist

The Crossover Twist, adapted from *Udarakarshanandasana*, is easy to practise. As your body loosens up, you can increase the stretch to greater effect by lowering your raised knee towards the floor.

Benefits include the freeing of tightness in the lower back, and relief from tiredness. The Twist also tones the hips and outer thighs, revitalizes the spine and refreshes the nervous system. Its abdominal massaging action relieves sluggish bowels and alleviates constipation. There are no special contraindications. Simply stop if the practice becomes uncomfortable, and do not stretch beyond your limits.

Your energetic focus is on *manipura chakra* (see page 17). Your imaginative thought might be: **'I am centred between past and future.'**

[1] Start by lying on the floor with your knees bent and your arms in a natural diagonal line away from your body, with the palms facing downwards. Support your neck with a rolled hand towel if required. **»** Raise your right foot onto your left thigh, placing the instep on the knee. Exhale, then inhale for a count of five as you elongate your spine along the floor.

1

[2] Exhale for a count of five, easing your supporting knee over to the left as far as is comfortable or you are able. As your leg crosses the plane of your body, support the thigh with your left hand. At the same time, bend your left knee and slide your left foot under the raised thigh, grasping it gently with your right hand. Ensure that the left knee is in line with the crown of your head. **»** Turn your head to the right, against the general twist. Your right hip will come off the floor but both shoulders should remain squarely on it.

» Breathe easily and naturally as you hold the position for a short while, making further small adjustments both to facilitate a good stretch and to make your body generally more comfortable. Do not strain or overstretch. Be patient, coaxing your body gently and protecting your baby at all times.

[3] Now unwind and return to the starting position. Take two or three natural breaths, then raise your left foot onto your right thigh or knee (see 3A), and repeat the sequence with the twist in the opposite direction (see 3B). **»** Return to the starting position and take two to three natural breaths.

[4] Winding down
To unwind, cross your right ankle over your left and pull the soles of your feet towards the backs of your thighs. Gently rock from side to side, massaging the lower back muscles and stretching the ankles. Change feet and repeat, breathing naturally.

2

3A

3B

4

Hip Rotation

This hip rotation sequence produces similar effects to those derived from the classic Crow Walking (*Kawa Chalasana*), which can be rather hard on the joints. It will help to prevent stiffness in the hips, knees and ankles, massage the buttocks and break up fatty tissue, improve blood circulation in the legs, massage the abdomen and alleviate constipation. It will also prepare the practitioner for seated postures such as the Lotus (*Padmasana*).

There is no particular energetic focus for this sequence, so watch your breath carefully and work smoothly with the movements. Your imaginative thought might be:
'I am rooted in the earth and my loving prayers fly to heaven.'

Safety note
Do not practise this sequence if you suffer from weak ankles or have had a recent sprain. Do not practise on a hard floor or surface, and provide plenty of cushioning protection for the coccyx.

[1] Sit in 'attitude' with your left heel pulled closely into the pubis or, as an easier option, the ball of the foot pointing towards the knee. The right heel should be by the right hip. Place your fingertips on the floor behind you to help support the aligned spine, and to expand the chest and pull back the shoulders.

[2] Breathing naturally, lean back slightly, taking your weight onto your hands. Raise your left knee so that the shin is vertical to the floor. Allow your right knee to lift slightly to accommodate the movement. Inhale slowly.

[3] Exhale as you turn your whole body clockwise to the right and towards the right back foot, approximately 180 degrees, to face the opposite way. The right knee rotates outwards until it touches the floor whilst the left knee rotates inwards to a 45-degree angle. Inhale as you rotate your body upright and exhale as you complete the 180-degree rotation to the opposite side.
» Repeat the rotation, synchronized with your breathing, six times on each side.

[4] Return to the starting position, sitting in 'attitude'. Gently bring your palms together near your heart.

[5] Inhale slowly as you raise your hands to touch momentarily above your head,

[6] Continuing the same long inhalation up into the final stretch with your arms extended fully above your head. » Exhale with a long, controlled breath, touching your palms to the top of the head before returning them, as you complete the exhalation, to their position in front of the heart. Repeat this part of the sequence six times, synchronizing it carefully with your breathing.

Blossoming Lotus

'Fine art is that in which the hand, the head and the heart go together,' said the nineteenth-century English art critic John Ruskin. In this Blossoming Lotus series, which I have developed over the years, the hands are the opening lotus petals; the head is the blossoming flower; and the heart is the stem. Together they tell the story of the developing pregnancy and its joyful conclusion.

On a physical level, the sequence works on the ankles, knees and hips, opens the chest and lungs and promotes an elegant and graceful body. You may keep the Hip Rotation starting position as a base for this sequence (see page 46).

Your energetic focus will start at the feet (roots) and the basal chakras (*mooladhara* and *swadhistana*) and rise through the chakras as the movements progress to full flowering at *Sahasrara* – the thousand-petalled lotus (at the crown of the head).

Your imaginative thought might be: ***'I hold the world in my arms.'***

Safety note
If you suffer from varicose veins, cartilage problems or low blood pressure, do not use the seated position (illustrated), but keep the Hip Rotation starting position ('attitude', see page 46) as a base for this sequence.

[1] Starting position
Kneel astride a cushion or firm, rolled bath towel, raising your heels and flexing your toes. Inhale and, taking the weight on your fingers, slowly walk your hands backwards.

[2] Exhale as you come upright to sit on the towel or cushion. If you are flexible enough, remove the support and sit between your feet. Gently bring your palms together near your heart.

[3] Exhale, then inhale, raising your hands to touch momentarily above your head.

[4] Continue the same long inhalation up into the final position, a full extension right above your head.

[5] Exhale as you gracefully arc your hands in a complete circle, bringing them to rest in the baby-cradling position. **»** Working gently and breathing evenly, repeat the whole sequence twice more.

[6] Winding down
At this point you may wish to rearrange your feet by returning to the starting position and releasing them from their flexed position. Relieve the pressure on the balls of your feet by turning the soles uppermost. Sit back once again between your feet, either onto the rolled towel or your calves. Close your eyes, breathing naturally.

1

2

3

4

5

6

The Cat

Everyone loves this posture, *Marjariasana*. Because of its raised-back form, some people think of it as an angry cat, but I prefer to perceive it as an awakening one. The *asana* (posture) improves the flexibility of the neck, shoulders and spine. It gently tones the reproductive system and can be safely practised (suitably modified) up to the sixth month of pregnancy. All the contractions are performed very gently, to coax rather than force. It has the added benefit of toning the upper arms.

Your energetic focus is on *swadhistana chakra*. Your imaginative thought might be: **'I am luxuriating in my flexibility.'**

Safety note
Whilst performing *Marjariasana*, it is not advisable to allow your back to become strongly concave (hollow) because the weight of the baby can cause your back muscles to strain.

[1] Starting position
Kneel, then lower yourself to rest on your forearms. Your thighs and upper arms should be vertical with your knees in line with your hips. Look towards the floor.

1

2

[2] Come up onto all fours, extending your elbows and pressing your inner biceps forwards. Distribute your weight evenly and make sure the crown of your head is in line with your tailbone. When in this position, keep your elbows locked to maintain a strong body framework. Pause for two to three natural breaths before repeating a further five times.

[3] Inhale, then exhale for a count of five, lowering your head with your chin pointing towards your chest. Contract the buttocks and push the hips forwards, curving the spine in a convex manner, and rise onto the fingertips to create the maximum stretch in the neck and shoulders. » Inhale slowly as you release the posture, reversing the movement down to the previous position (see 2). Pause for two to three natural breaths before repeating a further five times.

[4] Winding down
Wind down by sitting back on your feet, knees open, and leaning on your elbows with your chin cupped in your hands. Hold the position for two to three natural breaths.

3

4

The Camel

The Camel, *Ushtrasana*, is a strong stretch so I have adapted it for use with one or two chairs during pregnancy. It mobilizes the shoulders and can correct rounded and drooping ones – the curse of office workers. The spine is well flexed in this posture, and the nerves stimulated. The Camel also stretches the stomach and intestines, can alleviate constipation and has a regulating effect on the thyroid.

Your energetic focus is on *swadhistana* or *vishuddhi chakra*. Your imaginative thought might be:
'Peace comes when I follow total action with total stillness.'

[1] Starting position
Kneel comfortably between two chairs with your legs hip-width apart and your feet pointing in towards each other. Your big toes must touch to stabilize the movement and your buttocks should be contracted to strengthen the back muscles. For safety, place the chair behind you against a wall. If you need it for support, hold onto the leading edge of the second chair.

[2] Inhale, then exhale for a count of five, moving your hands back to hold onto the back chair legs or seat, arching your body while still looking forwards.

[3] Inhale, then exhale for a count of five, arching your head back to achieve your maximum comfortable stretch. Hold the static stretch for two to three natural breaths or longer.
» Inhale as you bring your head forwards and return to the upright starting position to release the stretch. » Repeat the whole sequence three times, holding as long as comfortable.

[4] Winding down
When you have completed your three repetitions, come into the winding-down position. Sit back on your feet, knees open, with your head resting on your forearms at the leading edge of the front chair. » Alternatively, rest your elbows on the floor and cup your forehead in your hands. Hold the position for two to three natural breaths.

1

2

3

4

Stretching and Lengthening

This sequence requires two chairs and is designed to stretch and lengthen your spine in preparation for the progressively stronger stretches. You may find your balance being affected by your pregnancy and using a chair will help to stabilize this problem. It is important to note that you should stretch the spine upwards before you perform any twisting actions. The following sequence can be performed either as separate exercises or they can flow from one to another.

Your imaginative thought might be: *'Even when I am seemingly doing nothing, I am still strengthening, learning and training.'*

1

Safety note
If you have high blood pressure, do not fold completely forwards in the final step. Instead, lean on your legs and simply relax your head.

[1] Starting position

Sit upright with the base of your spine against the chair back, legs hip-width apart, hands resting on your upper thighs. » Exhale, drawing the abdomen in slightly. Inhale for a count of five, raising your arms over your head in line with your shoulders, palms facing each other. » Exhale for a count of one to five, lowering your arms to the Starting Position. Repeat a further five times, ensuring that you elongate your spine and keep your shoulders down.

[2] From the Starting Position of step 1, inhale for a count of one to five, then exhale for a count of five, twisting to your right while keeping your spine straight but not rigid. Your right arm and hand remain relaxed over the chair back, while your left hand levers against your right knee to twist the top of the torso as far round as possible. » Hold the position for two to three natural breaths. Inhale as you turn to face forwards again. » Exhale and reverse the position, twisting around to the left and holding for two to three natural breaths. Repeat the twist to each side two more times.

[3] To provide an even stronger stretch, sit sideways on your chair with the chair back to your right. Grasping it with both hands, inhale, then exhale twisting your upper torso from the waist around to the right. Your right hand performs a pushing action and your left a pulling one. Perform this twist in a slowly executed and smooth movement. Turn your head to go with the flow of the twist, with your chin at right angles to the chest while your shoulders remain level. The aim is to balance the crown of your head above the base of the spine. **»** Once in the final position, hold for two to three natural breaths. Inhale and slowly return to the centre position. **»** Turn yourself on the seat so that the chair back is on your left. Inhale before exhaling and repeating the twist movement to the reverse side.

[4] As a counterstretch to the twist and to rest your back in a forward-facing position, lengthen the spine by bending from your hips and resting your relaxed hands on the chair back or seat in front of you. **»** Allow your head to relax between your arms as your back lengthens. Breathe naturally whilst in this position.

[5] Winding down
Relax forwards, curling your head, neck and spine until your hands touch the ground, as if you are a floppy rag doll. If you cannot manage this, lean your forearms on your splayed knees or thighs. Allow the full weight of your head to pull out any tension in your spine. Rest for several natural breaths or longer.

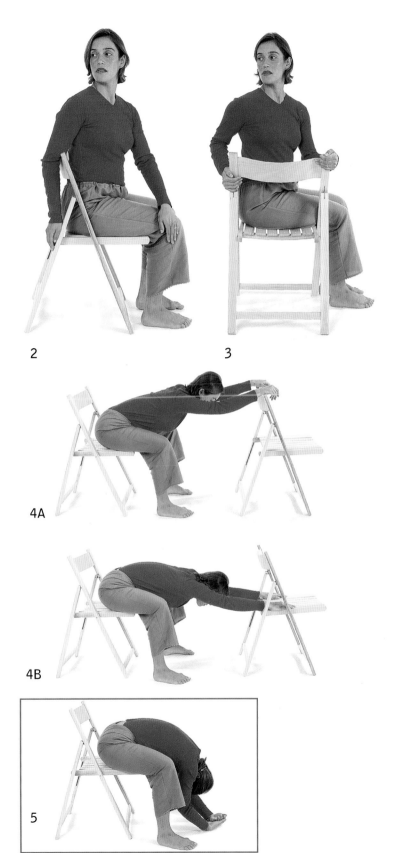

2

3

4A

4B

5

The Monkey Stretch

Hanuman, the monkey-chief, hero of the Hindu epic the *Ramayana*, was renowned for his courage, devotion, strength, flexibility, will and power. These qualities are reflected in the posture that bears his name, *Hanumanasana*. The classical version, which is essentially the full 'splits' as performed by ballet dancers, is frankly not achievable by most Westerners, so I have adapted the posture for both safety and efficacy.

Hanumanasana is hugely beneficial in loosening the hip muscles and opening the pelvic girdle. It can ease lower back pain, tones the muscles around the buttocks and massages the abdomen. Practised regularly, it is one of the best ways of ensuring a youthful body into old age.

Your energetic focus can be on either *mooladhara chakra* at the base of the spine, *anahata chakra* at the heart or *ajna chakra*, the Third Eye. Your imaginative thought might be: **'It's working; I can see the results.'**

[1] Starting position
Kneel on all fours and totally relax the right hip and leg. Breathing naturally, slide the right leg back, keeping the knee on the ground, and lowering the hips towards the left foot.

[2] Exhale as your relaxed right leg slides back until it reaches its maximum stretch, and your left buttock comes to rest on your left foot which is lying flat on the floor. ❯❯ Pull your hands and arms back towards your body so that you can keep a balanced, upright carriage. Keep your eyes softly focused forwards.

1

2

3

4

5

6

[3] Inhale for a count of five as you lift and rotate your head and gaze in a circle to your maximum comfortable stretch. **»** Exhale as you unwind from the position and return to all fours. Reverse the position, sliding your left leg backwards. Repeat the whole practice, left and right, three times.

[4] From the all-fours position and breathing naturally, place your left foot between your arms, resting your inner thigh on the outer side of the ribcage. Keeping your hips square, push your pelvis forwards to its maximum stretch.

[5] Inhale for a count of five, balancing with your palms together near your heart. Exhale, pushing a little bit further into the lunge.

[6] Inhale for a count of five, slowly and fully extending your arms above your head. **»** Hold momentarily and then exhale, reversing back down onto all fours. Repeat the whole practice, left and right, three times.

[7] Winding down
Relax for a while on your back in *Savasana*, the Corpse Posture, with your knees bent, breathing naturally.

7

Bamboo Balance

This series is more elegant and graceful than using a chair, although no less effective. Bamboo, as both prop and symbol used in the following two series, is strong and supportive yet light and flexible – a fine analogy of the spine itself. I have simply fashioned a bamboo staff from three garden bean-poles – simple but effective.

Bamboo Balance will improve focus, concentration and poise. It limbers all the joints and tones deep-seated muscles in the legs.

Your energetic focus is on *anahata* at the heart. Your imaginative thought might be: **'I am strong and flexible, yet move lightly as a reed.'**

Safety note
If you have weak joints or cartilage problems, you may have to limit yourself to the half-squat position until your tolerance and efficiency improves.

1

2

3

[1] Stand in *Tadasana*, the Mountain Posture (see page 23), holding your canes at the level of your navel.

[2] Exhale, then inhale for a count of five, rising onto the balls of your feet, locking your heels, ankles, knees and hips together as you extend upwards.

[3] Exhale for a count of five as you bend into a half-squat. **»** Hold momentarily and inhale for a count of five.

[4] Exhale for a count of five as you sit into a full squat, sitting on both heels and allowing the knees to open to accommodate your baby. **»** Inhale for a count of five as, using the power of your thigh muscles, you rise in a controlled manner to your full height (see step 2). Gear your upward movement exactly with your breath. Do not rise too quickly if you suffer from low blood pressure and, if you feel any dizziness, pause until the feeling passes. Repeat the whole series at least two more times.

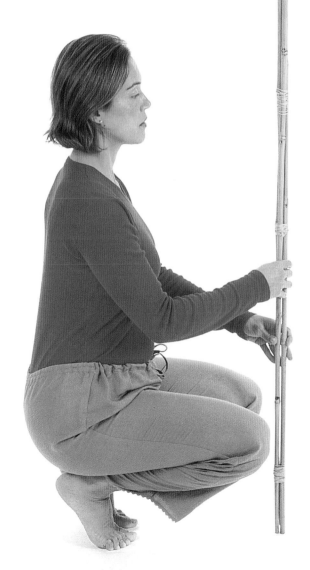

4

Bamboo Stretch

Based on the Right Angle Pose (*Samakonasana*), this sequence is excellent for stretching the hamstrings, working on the upper back and correcting spinal curvature. Even if you suffer from sciatica or have a bad back, you can perform the supported version with the aid of the bamboo canes. Once your legs are comfortably set apart and the heels turned slightly out and toes slightly in, it is one of the safest way to work.

Your energetic focus is on *anahata* at the heart or *manipura chakra*, your emotional centre at the navel. Your imaginative thought might be: **'I am the present unfolding.'**

[1] Starting position
Stand in *Tadasana*, the Mountain Posture (see page 23), holding the bamboo canes at the level of your navel. Breathing naturally, slowly walk away from the canes, bending your knees whilst keeping your head in a natural alignment with your hips. Allow your body to unfold forwards.

[2] To create the full stretch, walk further away and straighten your legs to form a right-angle with your body. Use each exhalation of the natural breath to help you achieve a greater stretch. Breathe out any discomfort. Hold for two to three natural breaths.

[3] Move slightly closer to the canes and take a hand position a little higher than before. Spread the feet to a comfortable position and bend the elbows and knees to prevent strain on your back. Angle your toes towards the canes, with the heels pointing outwards, to help open the hips.

[4] Slowly straighten your knees and extend your body to its maximum forward stretch. Hold for two to three natural breaths. Release the stretch. Slowly walk up the canes to assume the starting position (see step 1) and repeat the whole sequence twice more.

[5] Winding down
Relax in a casual standing posture using the canes for support.

1

2

3

4

5

Standing Twist

Unless they are fairly advanced students, pregnant women should not practise floor-seated spiral twists as they create too much pressure around the baby. This sequence is a version of the spinal twist (*Meru Wakrasana*) yet maintains the vertical line of the Mountain Posture (*Tadasana*).

In general, twisting postures not only work on the flexibility and health of the back muscles, but also massage the abdomen and vital organs. This revitalizing and rejuvenating action also extends to one's emotional life, releasing knots and tensions created by upset and unresolved conflicts.

Your energetic focus is on *manipura chakra* – the seat of the emotions around the navel. Your imaginative thought might be:
'I am untying the knots that entangle my life.'

Safety note
Do not practise this posture if you suffer from severe back problems, ulcers or hernias.

[1] Stand in *Tadasana*, Mountain Posture (see page 23), facing a chair. Raise your right leg and place your foot squarely on the chair seat, opposite your right hip. Inhale for a count of five as you stretch up through the spine, pulling the weight off your supporting left hip.

[2] Place your right palm over the base of the spine and your left palm on the outer edge of the right knee. Exhale for a count of five as you twist and turn to your right, using your left hand as a lever to assist the stretch. Allow your head to turn with the movement to look over your right shoulder while your hips remain square to the chair.
» Hold momentarily, then inhale as you turn to face front and exhale, returning to the standing *Tadasana*.

[3] Reverse the position by placing your left foot on the chair seat and twisting in the opposite direction. **»** Return to the standing *Tadasana* and repeat the whole sequence two further times on each side.

[4] Stand with your legs comfortably apart, heels turned slightly outwards and toes slightly inwards. Place your right palm over the base of your spine and your left palm to cradle the right hip. **»** Inhale, then exhale for a count of five as you twist to the right, keeping the pelvis square to the front. Hold momentarily, then inhale as you turn to face the front and exhale as you return to the standing *Tadasana*.
» Reverse the standing twist, turning to the left, and repeat the sequence two more times to each side.

» Variation Try the same standing twist with your feet together and your ankles, knees and hips locked. Twisting the top half of the torso gives an even stronger stretch.

[5] Winding down
Finally, rest in *Tadasana* for a few natural breaths.

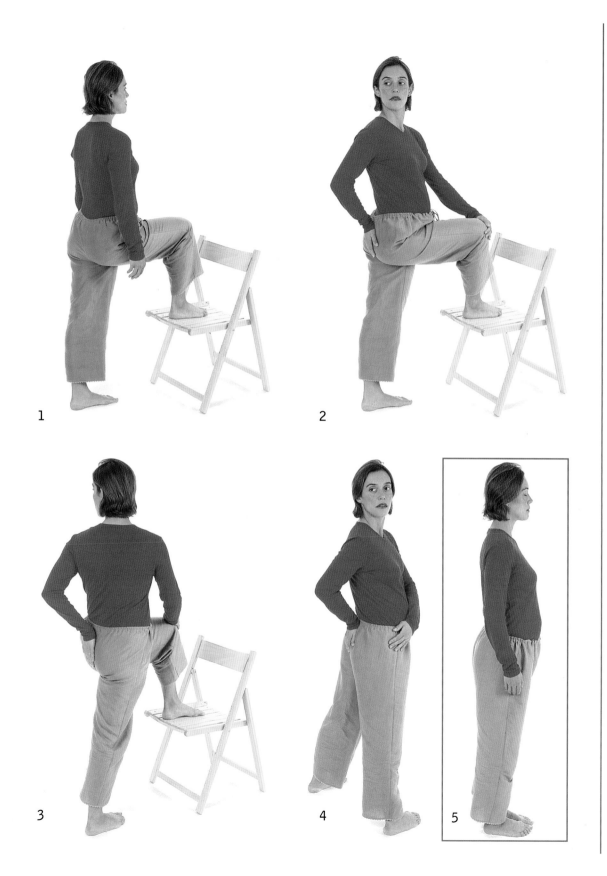

1

2

3

4

5

Sun Breathing

Safety note
Do not practise this breathing technique for at least half an hour after eating food as it may interfere with digestion.

Although an important practice in its own right, Sun Breathing or *Surya Bheda Pranayama*, vitality stimulating breath, is a useful prelude to *Nadi Shodhana Pranayama*, which offers the best opportunity to experience the full range of psychic network purification (see pages 92–3). The complete practice of Sun Breathing requires the use of *bandhas* or locks to be fully effective, but this would not be recommended during pregnancy.

Sun Breathing has some very useful benefits for the mother-to-be, including a notable ability to create heat in the body, and can boost the efficiency of any physical activity. If you feel dull or lethargic it will make the mind more alert and perceptive, increase extroversion and dynamism and help to alleviate depression. Psychically, it has a purifying effect on *pingala nadi*, the solar or masculine channel of the psychic network (see pages 16–7).

>> Sit in a comfortable meditational posture, that is one that enables the spine to remain as straight as possible without strain. If your ligaments are flexible enough, sit in a crosslegged position such as *Padmasana*, the Lotus, or half-Lotus, with your base vertebra directly on the floor or supported by a cushion (see page 65). Otherwise, sit comfortably on a straight-backed chair. If you wish, rest your right hand on your knee in *Chin Mudra*, the psychic gesture of consciousness. *Chin Mudra* is one of a number of psycho-neural finger-locks that make meditation *asanas* (postures) more powerful.

>> Close your eyes and relax your whole body, breathing naturally until you feel calm and composed. Raise your left hand and place the thumb gently against your left nostril. Inhale slowly and fully through the right nostril. Gently close the right nostril with the ring finger of your left hand. When both nostrils are gently sealed, retain the breath for as long as is comfortable. >> When you are ready, release the seal on the right nostril and, still closing the left nostril with the thumb, exhale slowly and fully through the right nostril. This is one round. >> For novice practitioners, ten rounds would be sufficient as an introduction. As you become more proficient the practice may be extended to three to five minutes.

Moon Breathing

Moon Breathing, or *Chandra Bhedana Pranayama*, vitality cooling breath, is the complementary opposite of Sun Breathing. Its effects on the body are cooling and calming, both physically and psychologically. A physically overactive system can be soothed and tempered, the mind quietened and encouraged to become more introspective. *Chandra Bhedana* has its primary effect on *ida nadi*, the female aspect of the psychic network (see pages 16–7).

The procedure and technique are the same as for Sun Breathing except that the hands and nostril directions are reversed.

Safety note
These two *pranayamas* should not be practised together on the same day. They exert very different physical, emotional, mental and psychic effects, so should only be applied to address a particular need.

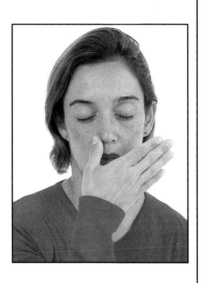

» Sit in a comfortable meditational posture, such as *Padmasana*, the Lotus, or half-Lotus, with your base vertebra directly on the floor or supported by a cushion (see below left). Otherwise, sit comfortably on a straight-backed chair. If you wish, rest your right hand on your knee in *Chin Mudra*, the psychic gesture of consciousness. *Chin Mudra* is one of a number of psycho-neural finger-locks that make meditation *asanas* (postures) more powerful.

» Raise your right hand and place the thumb gently against your right nostril closing it. Inhale slowly and fully through your left nostril. Gently close the left nostril with the ring finger of your right hand. When both nostrils are sealed, retain the breath for as long as is comfortable. When you are ready, release the seal on the left nostril and, still closing the right nostril with the thumb, exhale slowly and fully through the left nostril. This is one round.
» For novice practitioners, ten rounds would be sufficient as an introduction. As you become more proficient the practice may be extended to three to five minutes.

Mid-Pregnancy

The Second Trimester

14–30 weeks

Baby's skin is thin and shiny with no underlying fat.

Finger- and toe-prints are visible.

Eyelids begin to part and the eyes open.

You will feel your baby moving between 18 and 22 weeks if this is your first pregnancy, or earlier if it is your second. The baby has really been moving since he or she was two months old.

By five months your baby can hear your voice, so talk, sing or play your favourite music for him/her to hear.

By six months, your baby's eyes can open and distinguish light and dark.

By the end of the sixth month, your baby is 33 cm (13 inches) long and weighs about 675 g (1½ lb).

Your children are not your children.
They are the sons and daughters of Life's longing for itself.
They come through you but not from you,
And though they are with you yet they belong not to you.

You may give them your love but not your thoughts,
For they have their own thoughts.
You may house their bodies but not their souls,
For their souls dwell in the house of tomorrow,
Which you cannot visit, not even in your dreams.
You may strive to be like them but seek not to make them like you.

From The Prophet, *Kahlil Gibran*

Natural Home Health Help

The second trimester of pregnancy (14–30 weeks) is often referred to as the 'blooming time'. By now your body will have weathered the first set of changes and will be settling down a little. As you can imagine, however, this period is not without its potential discomforts.

Cramps

The prolonged contraction of a group of muscles produces the severe pain known as cramp. This is usually located in the calves, thighs, buttocks, neck and lower back. It is more common in hot weather, after intense physical activity and at night when the muscles are tired. It occurs intermittently and is more discomforting than serious. Postural imbalance is probably the most common contributory cause. Wearing high heels is another.

• Increased salt intake – this should be natural sea salt – in hot weather may cure the problem but avoid salt if you have raised blood pressure.

• 'Rise and fall' exercises with the bamboo cane (see Bamboo Balance and Bamboo Stretch, pages 58–61) before you go to bed are recommended.

• Try raising your mattress slightly at the foot end to help improve your circulation.

Dizziness and fainting

This can be caused simply by trying to do too much – you should never work until you are exhausted. It can also be due to lowered blood pressure or low blood sugar. You may even feel faint just before a meal.

• Do not stand or sit for too long or get up too quickly, and don't lie flat on your back – it just doesn't suit people who have either low or high blood pressure.

• Use the postural exercises (see Posture, Poise and Balance, pages 22–3) regularly.

• Avoid smoky atmospheres.

• Avoid tightly fitting clothes, shoes and jewellery – anything that restricts blood flow.

• Keep some barley sugar sweets to hand to provide an instant blood sugar lift if you feel dizzy, and peppermints to help relieve symptoms of nausea.

• Revive yourself by smelling an aromatherapy oil sprinkled on a handkerchief.

Constipation

As a result of the extra hormones produced when pregnant, the intestines tend to relax and become less efficient. Regular Yoga practice will prevent this problem occurring, but there are other preventive tricks you can try as well.

• Start your day by sipping a cup of hot water (unless you have high blood pressure, in which case it should be cold).

• Make sure you have breakfast – the first and best meal of the day – as it plays a key role in keeping the bowels moving.

• Eat very ripe bananas (under-ripe for diarrhoea) or soaked prunes, fresh plums, apples (unless you suffer indigestion), pears, mangoes, papaya and pineapple. These are excellent fruits, especially combined with a rice or oat cereal.

• Eat regular meals that include the following: leeks, beetroot, peeled fresh tomatoes, spring cabbage, Chinese leaf, rocket, watercress, lettuce and celery.

- Eat a different cereal or pulse every day, for example, lentils, barley, brown rice, couscous.

- Limit your intake of wheat products, eggs and cheese, as they can bind the system.

- Drink plenty of mineral water, preferably uncarbonated, during the day.

- Give yourself plenty of time to evacuate the bowels and put your feet up when eating your breakfast – it is amazing how effective this is.

- If constipation leads to the misery of piles (haemorrhoids), these can be soothed by the local application of witch hazel.

Varicose veins

The same hormones that contribute to constipation effect the elasticity of the veins, causing them to become varicose. Other causes include: sitting with crossed legs; wearing tightly fitting clothes and poorly fitting shoes, restrictive underwear, socks and stockings; and suffering from a lack of exercise, all of which ultimately block up the whole system.

- Keep your body moving – don't treat pregnancy as an ailment.

- Do not allow your body to stagnate, so avoid sitting or standing in one place for too long.

Tingling and numbness in the hands

This is caused by pressure on the nerves and tendons caused by swelling of the hands and wrists, known as Carpal Tunnel Syndrome. To relieve or avoid the problem, try the following simple remedies.

- Remove any tight jewellery you may be wearing and perhaps put your rings on a chain for the time being.

- Take your watch off – who needs time anyway?

- In your antenatal exercises, make sure that you include those in which your arms are raised above your head.

- Use self-help massage (see Self-Massage, pages 104–7) to work on your lymphatic drainage.

The Supported Bridge

This is a complete tonic for the whole system and enables you to do more by doing less! A warm-up for the more classical postures that follow, the sequence can be made as easy or hard-working as you wish. Our illustrations depict the easier option, using a rolled bath towel or firm blanket beneath the small of the back. To increase the stretch, you can add a pillow on top of the roll to run along the length of your torso. This will open your chest, ribcage and abdomen to an even greater extent. The sequence is suitable for virtually every pregnant mother as long it is not overdone. You must decide what level of support suits your capabilities.

The Supported Bridge can help to alleviate backache and refresh the spinal nerves. It will also work on the digestive system, preventing and easing indigestion. Psychologically it creates a sense of space in the body and soothes and supports your emotional centre, in the area of the navel.

Concentration and mental awareness of a chakra or psychic energy node greatly improves the understanding and effectiveness. For this sequence, your energetic focus is on *manipura chakra*, around the navel. Your imaginative thought might be: **'I have space to grow.'**

[1] Starting position

Lie on the floor, supporting your head with a pillow. Starting with your knees bent and legs comfortably apart, raise your hips and slide a rolled bath towel or blanket under the small of the back. » Carefully lower your body down, making sure that your hips are firmly and squarely on the floor. Mould your body around the shape of the roll. » Once you are comfortable, place your hands on your hips. Stay in this position for a few natural breaths, relaxing your torso and extending your muscles.

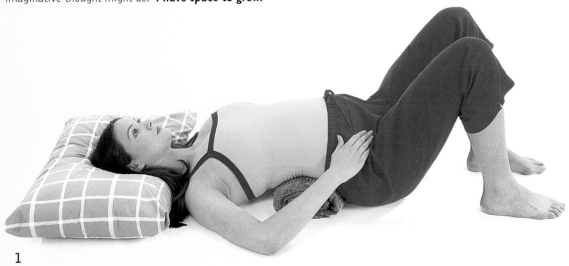

1

[2] Exhale, then inhale for a count of five as you take your arms gracefully over your head and rest the backs of your hands either on the pillow or the floor. Relax once more into the position, breathing naturally and allowing the muscles to let go even further.

2

[3] Inhale, then exhale for a count of five as you open your knees to form a diamond shape and bring the soles of your feet together. **»** Relax once again as you breathe naturally, feeling the increased level of stretch.

3

[4] Inhale, then exhale for a count of five as you slowly extend your legs and allow them to fall open from the hips. Breathe naturally as you accommodate this new stretch.

Winding down

As a winding-down movement, return to the starting position (see step 1), and remove the rolled bath towel or blanket from under the small of your back. Keep your knees bent up and feel the whole length of your spine relaxing along the floor. Breathe naturally for a while.

4

Spiral Twist

This Spiral Twist, adapted from *Jathara Parivartanasana*, gives a wonderful internal massage to the stomach and internal organs. It can ease indigestion and sluggish bowels as well as alleviate constipation. It also works on the spinal muscles and nerves.

Your energetic focus is on *manipura chakra*, the centre of the emotions. Your imaginative thought might be: **'I will let go of fear.'**

[1] Lie on the floor, supporting your head and shoulders with two pillows, one along the spine and the other under the head, and have your knees bent and legs together. **»** Spread your arms out to the sides at a 45-degree angle from your body to provide a stabilizing framework.

[2] Inhale, then exhale for a count of five as you roll your legs up and over to the right, still keeping them bent. Cradle under the knees with your right arm, elbow on the floor, to form a strong supporting framework. As your knees move to the right, twist your head gently to the left to form a spiral shape along your spine. Remain in the twist and breathe naturally for two to three breaths. **»** Inhale for a count of five as you come back to the central position.

[3] Exhale as you repeat the twist to the opposite side. Repeat slowly a further two times to either side.

[4] Winding down
Wind down with your hands cradling the baby and your ankles crossed, feet flat on the floor. Breathe naturally as you feel your spinal muscles relax.

1

2

3

4

The Crossover Twist

This sequence is adapted from The Crossover Twist on pages 44–5 to make it is easier to perform now that your baby is growing bigger and you need more space. It is also suitable for the latter part of your pregnancy.

It provides a slightly stronger stretch than the previous spinal twist and, by extending one leg, offers even more relief for backache. It will also help to tone the outer thigh and hip muscles. Regular practice will stop you feeling lethargic. You may wish to take the precaution of having some small cushions handy to support your knees in the twist.

Your energetic focus is on *manipura chakra* around the navel. Your imaginative thought might be: *'I will let go of fear and prejudice.'*

[1] Starting position
Lie on the floor, your head and shoulders still supported by two pillows. Extend your legs, shoulder-width apart. Angle your arms away from your body at a 45-degree angle and use them as levers during the practice. Press your shoulders towards the floor throughout the sequence.

[2] Exhale, then inhale for a count of five, drawing the right foot along the extended left leg to rest the instep just over the left knee.

1

2

[3] Exhale for a count of five as you ease the right knee over to the left side, either coming to rest on a cushion or making contact with the floor. At the same time turn your head slowly in the opposite direction to create the twist. Hold for two to three natural breaths, feeling the lengthening of the spine and the toning effect on the back and leg muscles. You are endeavouring to maintain a straight line from the heel of the foot to the crown of the head. ➤➤ Inhale for a count of five as you come back to the central position.

[4] Exhale as you repeat the twist to the opposite side. Repeat the whole sequence slowly, a further two times to either side.

[5] Winding down

Wind down by resting with the outside of your feet touching on a rolled towel or pillow, knees bent outwards and hands cradling your baby. Breathe naturally as you feel your spine settling into the floor.

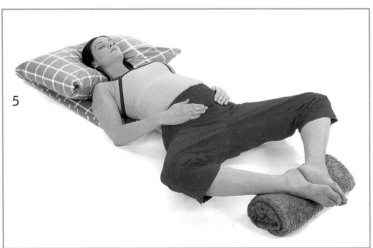

The Wave

One form of exercise that most pregnant women love is swimming, which is a perfect complement to Yoga. The Wave is equally effective at getting the spine moving in a wave-like action to bring a sense of fluidity. In this sequence, the practices can be blended dynamically and rhythmically, one posture into another. The fluidity of the movement can be judged by the action of the head. It takes the movement forwards, down towards the floor, curls in as the body leans back and unfolds and arcs backwards as the spine unfolds. Regular practice makes your spine and hips more elastic.

All the chakras are effectively stimulated by this sequence so your focus can rotate from psychic centre to psychic centre as the practice progresses. Your imaginative thought might be: *'Life flows through me.'*

[1] Sit on a cushion with your head, neck and spine in as straight line as possible without strain. With your knees bent forming an easy diamond shape, place the soles of your feet together and rest your hands on your knees.

[2] Inhale, then exhale as you ease forwards as far as is comfortable, holding your legs near the ankles to help lever the body gently towards the floor. The maximum position is with your head touching the feet and baby on the floor!

1

2

3

4

5

6

[3] Continuing the same exhalation, roll back the spine and tuck in your head, slowly sliding your hands back up to your knees.

[4] Still exhaling, lean back into the pelvis to your maximum stretch, chin to chest, holding your knees for support.

[5] As you inhale, imagine drawing in your breath from the base of the spine. To create the wave-like action, tilt the pelvis forwards and roll the spine backwards, opening the chest. **»** Still inhaling, complete the movement by pulling on the knees and arching your spine, neck and head backwards to your maximum stretch. **»** From the next breath, repeat the sequence a further five times.

[6] Winding down
Sit with one leg crossed in front of the other, cradling around your raised legs. Hold the position for a few natural breaths.

Rocking the Cradle

Rocking from side to side or round in a circle has long been accepted as a human comfort, so your baby will love this one, especially if you accompany it with your favourite music. Recent research has shown that music played to a baby in the womb is recognized and enjoyed by the infant in the outside world. It can be used to calm and reassure your baby, especially if it gets restless.

Additional benefits include a toning effect on the buttocks, helping to keep the pull of gravity at bay, and a loosening of the hip sockets. The final position, 'rocking the baby' (see step 4), also tones the muscles of the outer thigh which are usually so difficult to work on.

Your energetic focus is on *mooladhara chakra* (root centre) and *swadisthana chakra* (sexual centre) for the first three steps and *manipura chakra* at the navel for 'rocking the baby'. Your imaginative thought might be: **'Rock-a-bye Baby ...'**

[1] Sit on a cushion or firm folded blanket, with your head, neck and spine in as straight line as possible without straining (see 1A). Place the soles of the feet together and pull them towards your body so that, when you lean slightly forwards, your forearms lie along the insides of the calves (see 1B).

1A

1B

[2] Following your natural breath, rock over to the right, pressing your outer thigh into the floor and leaning your arms into your knees to keep your hips open.

[3] Use the impetus of the movement to rock over to the left. Repeat at least ten times to alternate sides.

[4] Now 'rock the baby'. Cradle your arms around one of your legs, as if you are holding your baby in your arms, tucking the foot into the crease of your opposite arm. Flex the leg in the hip socket with a semi-circular rocking motion around your baby bump. Repeat at least ten times, feeling an increasing stretch.
» Change legs and repeat the action with your other leg.

2

3

4

Balancing Posture

Balancing is a form of harmonization. Most people are extremely inefficient in the use of their muscles and, by extension, in the various aspects of their daily lives. True grace and poise, then, is really a study in energy efficiency – of balancing effort and action. Through training and practice one can learn to expend the minimum amount of effort for the maximum benefit.

It is often recommended that a Yoga session ends with some form of balancing posture, as it is an excellent preparation for the practices of *pranayama*, relaxation or meditation. The following posture is known as *Santolanasana*, the Balancing Posture. Apart from its obvious benefits in terms of balance and equilibrium, it gives the hands and arms a workout which helps with the problem of Carpal Tunnel Syndrome.

Your energetic focus is on *manipura chakra*, the emotional centre. Your imaginative thought might be:
'I am perfectly balanced between my past and my future.'

Safety note
Do not practise this sequence on a slippery floor. Build up your progress with patient practice, veering on the side of caution in the final position.

[1] Starting position
Kneel on all fours with your feet flexed and your heels raised. Ensure that the lumbar portion of your spine is flat, your shoulders vertically above your wrists and your hips in line with your knees to create a box effect. Extend your inner elbows and lock your arms. Breathe naturally throughout this practice

1

[2] To limber your body into the movement, lock your hips by pushing them slightly forwards, using your shoulders as an axle.

[3] When you feel secure, raise your knees off the floor, locking your ankles, knees and hips to help strengthen the lumbar area. » Balance so that your body forms a diagonal line from the crown of your head to the heels. Continue breathing naturally and hold the position as long as you feel comfortable. » Return to the starting position, on all fours (see step 1), and repeat the sequence twice more.

2

3

The Bow

In this adaptation of the classical Bow Posture, *Dhanurasana*, the body emulates a flexible bow while the arms are the taut bowstring. The 'target' of relaxation is accomplished once you have completed the sequence and are resting in the winding-down position. Apart from the obvious toning and conditioning effect on the back muscles and tension-relieving potential for the shoulder area, *Dhanurasana* strongly massages the internal organs, glands and abdominal muscles. Its action of opening the chest helps to relieve respiratory conditions aggravated by poor posture and chronic tension.

Your energetic focus is on *manipura chakra* at the navel. Your imaginative thought might be: **'My arrows of inspiration seek ever-greater horizons.'**

Safety note
This posture should not be practised for at least three to four hours after a meal, or not at all if you have a hernia, ulcer or a serious back condition.

[1] Starting position
Kneel on all fours, with arms fully extended and the crown of your head in line with your hips. Make sure that the lumbar portion of your spine is flat, your shoulders are vertically above your wrists and your hips are above the knees to create a box effect. Extend your inner elbows and lock your arms.

[2] Raise and extend your left leg at hip level and hold for two to three natural breaths.

[3] Bend your left knee, extending the lower leg upwards, and hold for a further two to three breaths.

[4] Providing you feel balanced and secure, grasp your left foot with your right hand, and with a expansive inhalation, arch your body and push the left foot up and away from your back to extend your arm. Ensure that your shoulders remain square to the front, and that your elbow is fully extended. Hold the static position for as long as is comfortable, then exhale, lowering the leg to the starting position. » Inhale and stretch once more, holding onto the bent leg for as long as you can. Exhale as you lower the leg, inhale, then repeat the stretch once more before exhaling down to relax on all fours. Pause for some natural breaths as your body relaxes. Repeat the sequence three times with your right leg.

[5] Winding down
Wind down by sitting back on your heels or on a cushion. Cradle your head in your hands with the elbows on the floor. Rest for two to three minutes.

1

2

3

4

5

The Dog

An excellent counterstretch to the previous arching posture, this gentle back strengthener is a preparatory warm-up version of The Dog, *Svanasana*. It resembles a dog stretching as it gets on its feet after being curled up. I have used a chair for this posture, which must be placed firmly against a wall or non-movable furniture for safety's sake. This chair-supported version is very safe and there are no particular contraindications. If you feel confident and flexible enough to work on the floor, use the variation outlined below.

Since the back is horizontal, the internal organs are suspended as in an animal's posture which will provide relief from the usual downward effect of gravity. The back, neck and shoulders are stretched, toned and strengthened which will alleviate deep-seated tension if the sequence is practised regularly.

Your energetic focus is on *vishuddhi chakra* at the throat. Your imaginative thought might be: **'I am growing out of my spine.'**

[1] Stand behind a chair and fold your forearms onto the chair back, resting your forehead on your arms. Remain in this position for two to three natural breaths, easing out of your pelvis by moving your hips from side to side as a preparatory warm-up exercise.

[2] Hold onto the chair back and walk away to form a table-top right-angle with your arms and torso. Open your legs hip-width apart and your arms shoulder-width apart. Keep the crown of your head in line with the base of your spine. If necessary, bend your knees to help extend and flatten your back. Hold for two to three natural breaths.

[3] Walk your hands down towards the chair legs to gain a deeper, more angled stretch, keeping your chin in line with your chest and shoulders and armpits fully extended (see 3A). » Walk down as far as you can comfortably while walking your feet away from the chair to accommodate the inverted stretch (see 3B).

[4] To help the extension from the base of the hips, bring your heels together, turning your toes out and bending your knees into a deep diamond shape. Hold for two to three breaths, then reverse back up to the starting position. » Rest comfortably for two to three natural breaths. Repeat the sequence two times.

[5] **Variation**
To increase the stretch, adopt an all-fours kneeling position with your hands positioned immediately below your shoulders, fingers turned outwards, knees in line with the hips and feet flexed.

[6] Inhale, then exhale as you raise and extend your knees, straightening your legs as your body comes into an inverted 'V' shape. Push your heels outwards and down towards the floor to help open the hips. Use the heels of the hands to push the floor away, straighten the arms, extend the shoulder sockets and expand the armpits. Keep your head in alignment with your spine with your chin remaining at right angles to your chest. » Hold the stretch for two to three natural breaths as you ease your body into its maximum static stretch. Inhale as you relax the stretch and come back into the all-fours starting position. » Repeat the sequence two more times. Breathe naturally throughout. Wind down in the starting position.

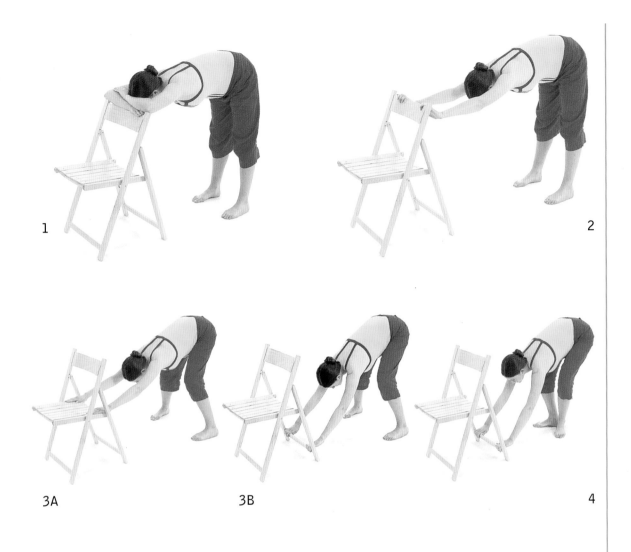

1

2

3A

3B

4

5

6

The Tree

These elegant postures, based on the classical Tree Pose, *Vrikshasana*, and One-Legged Prayer Pose, *Eka Pada Pranamasana*, are the epitome of poise and balance. Trees have consistent qualities of strength, vigorous durability, flexibility, rootedness and expansive growth. They have also long been planted as a way of commemorating the arrival of a new baby – in Switzerland, apple trees are planted for a girl and a nut tree for a boy. Choose your own tree imagery to accompany this sequence – the maidenly silver birch, the matronly beech, the powerful oak, for example.

As you practise, keep your breathing natural, unforced and unrestricted. If you feel any dizziness or your balance slipping, don't panic: gently drop your foot and arms and refocus your breath. For those not practised or confident enough to perform these positions without support, use a chair or, better still, a tree!

The Tree sequence tones the muscles, flexes and frees the joints, provides mental focus and improves poise and balance.

Your imaginative and energetic focus will range from the feet (roots) to the heart (trunk), the head/arms (branches) and the thoughts (fruits). Your imaginative thought might be: **'I am strong and flexible. I grow slowly and well. My roots are secure in life's enduring values.'**

Safety note
If you suffer from high blood pressure, do not hold your arms above your head for more than one breath.

1

[1] Stand with both feet together, your arms relaxed and your body upright in *Tadasana*, the Mountain Posture (see page 23). » Focus your gaze on a fixed point at eye level. Turn your toes out and bring your palms together, thumbs overlapping, at the sternum (breastbone).
» Working from the hip, turn your right knee to the side, raising your right heel to rest on the ball of the foot, touching the supporting ankle. Pull the weight off your supporting hip and level your pelvis. Become aware of your unforced heartbeat.

» Hold comfortably for a short while as you adjust to the balance.

[2] Slowly slide the right instep over the calf muscle on the inside of the supporting leg. Simultaneously raise your wrists onto the crown, opening the armpits and pushing the elbows back as far as possible. **»** Open the pelvis so that the right knee moves outwards in line with the plane of the hips and the way you are facing. Make sure that you are stretching up and off the supporting hip with your weight balanced evenly on the supporting foot. When you feel focused and well balanced, proceed to the next step.

[3] Use one hand to help raise the instep onto the side of your knee, or high up onto the inside of your inner thigh if you are capable. Bring your palms together again and raise your arms firstly above the crown as before. **»** Slowly extend your arms overhead to your maximum comfortable extension. When you feel focused and well-balanced, hold for two to three natural breaths.

2

3

The Stork

The stork is an elegant and graceful bird and has long been associated with the arrival of new babies. Adapted from the half-Lotus forward bend, *Ardha Baddha Padmottanasana*, The Stork is a simplified follow-on sequence from The Tree. It is excellent for opening out the hip joints and gives an overall stretch and tone as well as continuing the elements contained in a balancing programme.

The stretch to the legs and hip joints is slightly stronger than in The Tree, so the balance might be harder to maintain. There are two possible aids which you might wish to try if, at first, you are unsteady or unconfident in this kind of posture. Either stand with your back to a wall or rest your bent knee on a chair, using a firm, folded blanket to bring the seat to the appropriate height.

Your energetic focus is on *anahata chakra*, the heart centre. Your imaginative thought might be: **'I am waiting patiently.'**

Safety note
Do not practise this posture if you suffer from sciatica. If you suffer from high blood pressure, hold your arms stretched above your head for only one breath.

[1] Stand with both feet together, arms relaxed, and body upright in *Tadasana*, the Mountain Posture (see page 23). Focus your gaze on a fixed point at eye level.
>> Breathing naturally, cross your right foot over the left, pressing onto the ball of the foot to distribute your weight evenly between both feet. Bring your palms together near your heart. Hold for two to three breaths as you adjust to the balance.

1

[2] Raise your right foot into a position either just under or above the supporting left knee so you form a figure '4' shape. Pull back the left knee so it comes into line with the plane of your body. Inhale for a count of five as you slowly raise your hands to sit on the top of your head. Exhale, then breathe naturally as you adjust to the new balance.

[3] With the full support of your hands, increase the stretch on your ankle, knee and pelvic ligaments by raising the heel and outer edge of the right foot into the crease of the left thigh. Turn the sole uppermost, allowing the knee to turn both outwards and downwards as the foot moves towards the pelvis. The higher the foot, the lower the knee. Breathing naturally, adjust to the position.

[4] When you feel focused and well balanced, inhale for a count of five as you stretch your arms above your head. Hold for as long as you feel comfortable, breathing naturally. Exhale for a count of five as you lower your arms and place your hands first on top of your head, then at the heart centre. » Maintaining your balance, carefully and slowly release the bent leg. Stand in *Tadasana*, still with quietly focused gaze, until you feel ready to repeat the sequence on the other leg. » Wind down by standing comfortably in *Tadasana*.

2

3

4

Postures for Seated Meditation

An essential prerequisite for practising meditation is a comfortable, balanced and steady seat that will allow the body to remain still for extended periods. Additionally, the spine must be straight to allow the free flow of energies through the chakras. The practitioner must, therefore, strike a balance between achievable comfort and vigilant awareness, and this is not always easy. Achieving a comfortable cross-legged position can prove difficult for those used to sitting in chairs. Tight ligaments are the usual reason for an inability to open the legs for postures such as the Lotus (*Padmasana*) and, although pregnancy naturally softens pelvic ligaments, please be careful not to place undue strain on the knees (the weakest link in the chain) in your attempts to get into the final position.

Below, I outline some of the options achievable by most pregnant women and suggest that you try them all to find which will suit you best. When you have found your preferred posture, take a few minutes to adjust it, supported by pillows where necessary, in preparation for the Psychic Network Purification, *Nadi Shodhana*, which follows.

As you settle into your posture, your imaginative thought might be:
'I am perfectly still and peaceful.'

[1] Easy Posture

Sukhasana is the easiest of the meditational postures. The legs sit under the thighs and the hands rest either lightly on the knees or in a gesture such as *Gyana Mudra*, the psychic gesture of knowledge (as shown). **»** A pillow under the buttocks will help you achieve a comfortable sitting posture with your head, neck and spine in alignment.

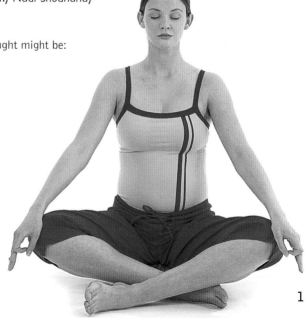

1

[2] Half-Lotus

Bend one leg and place the sole of the foot on the inside of the opposite thigh. Bend the other leg and place the foot as high as possible on top of the opposite thigh. The full Lotus is achieved when both feet are on top of their opposite thighs. This is an extremely stable *asana* that has an unrivalled reputation as the supreme meditation posture. If you practise the half-Lotus, ensure you strike a balance by using alternate raised legs. Don't always use your easiest or favoured side. The many benefits of the half-Lotus, or *Ardha Padmasana,* include a toning effect on the coccygeal and sacral nerves (which pass through the pelvic area) as the legs' blood flow is redirected to the abdominal area.

[3] Thunderbolt Posture

The *vajra* is one of the main *nadis* or psychic channels and regulates the body's sexual energy. This posture, *Vajrasana*, benefits the reproductive and digestive organs and is useful in the sublimation of sexual energy to the higher centres where it finds its expression in compassion, creative endeavour and wisdom.

» Kneel on the floor and lower your buttocks onto your feet, with your heels touching your hips. A pillow or meditation stool can relieve the pressure for those not used to sitting in such a position.

[4] Hero's Meditation Posture

Bend one leg under the other, with the heels touching the buttocks. Adjust one knee so that it is above the other. This posture, *Dyana Veerasana*, is easy to keep for long periods as a lot of the body is in contact with the floor.

2

3

4

Psychic Network Purification

This practice of *Nadi Shodhana* is a combination and extension of the practices of Sun and Moon Breathing (see pages 64–5). It is one of the best-loved and most widely-practised of the yogic *pranayamas*. It is particularly effective in centring and calming an overactive mind and stimulating and vitalizing a sluggish one.

If you check your breath, you will find that you breathe predominantly through one nostril rather than another. This changes throughout the day, the balance of restriction shifting from one nostril to the other every 20 to 90 minutes depending on an individual's body rhythms. When the right nostril is more open and the left brain is stimulated, we tend to engage in more outwardly orientated activities and think in a more logical, linear way. When the left nostril is more open and the right brain is stimulated, we engage in more introspective acts and think in a more holistic, pattern-sensing manner.

The practice of *Nadi Shodhana* balances the flow of air in both nostrils and achieves the rare facility of opening the central psychic channel, *Sushumna*. When this happens, we have access to a hugely increased energy current that refreshes and repairs our body, mind and spirit.

Nadi Shodhana can be practised in its most basic form: breathing in through the left nostril, and out through the right, in through the right, out through the left. Its full efficacy and potential, however, is realized when one works with the natural ratio of the breath (in for a count of two … hold in for a count of eight … exhale for a count of four … hold out for a count of four) and includes *bhandas* (locks that redirect *prana* – subtle energies – for the purpose of spiritual awakening). Get to know the basic pattern of breathing at first and, if you choose, use the easier count of three … nine … six to include the retention of the inhaled breath (*Antar Kumbhaka*) and, later still, the external retention (*Bahir Kumbhaka*) on a count of three … nine … six … six.

Various hand positions can be used for the practice. I have chosen *Nasagra Mudra*, the nosetip position. Depending on whether you are left- or right-handed, you may use your choice of hand. Support the elbow with your free hand if your arm gets tired. The descriptions of thumb and fingers utilize the right hand, so adjust for the left hand.

Sit in a comfortable meditational seated *asana*, or posture (see pages 90-1), or on a straight-backed chair which will allow you to remain still with your head, neck and spine in alignment.

[1] Bring your right hand up to the *Nasagra Mudra* position, fingertips relaxed and resting on the eyebrow centre. Press your thumb lightly against the right nostril, making a seal. Inhale slowly through the left nostril. Inhale for a count of three, using your beating heart as your pacemaker.

[2] Lightly pinch both nostrils closed and retain the breath internally momentarily, or for a count of nine.

[3] Release the thumb from the right nostril and exhale slowly, for a count of six if you wish.

[4] Lightly pinch both nostrils closed and retain the breath externally momentarily, or for a count of six.

[5] Release the thumb from the right nostril and inhale slowly, or for a count of three if you wish.

[6] Lightly pinch both nostrils closed and retain the breath internally momentarily, or for a count of nine.

[7] Release the ring finger from the left nostril and exhale slowly, or for a count of six.

[8] Lightly pinch both nostrils closed and retain the breath externally momentarily, or for a count of six.

This is one round. When first starting this practice, do no more than ten rounds. You may build it up, practising for 10–20 minutes or even longer as a meditation.

Late Pregnancy

The Third Trimester

30–40 weeks

Your baby's nails grow to the ends of the fingertips and beyond, the hair gets thicker and longer and the body is more rounded.

More confined and possibly engaged in the pelvis, your baby may be less active in preparation for the birth.

The baby's lungs are fully formed and mature.

At full term, your baby will be about 51 cm (20 inches) long and weigh 3.4 kg (7½ lb).

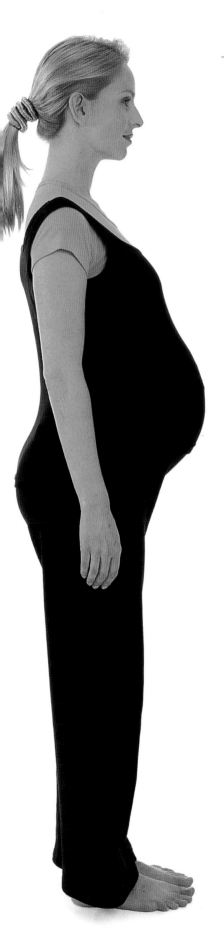

You are the bows from which your children as living arrows are sent forth.
The Archer sees the mark upon the path of the infinite, and He bends you with
His might that His arrows may go swift and far.
Let your bending in the Archer's hand be for gladness;
For even as He loves the arrow that flies, so He loves the bow that is stable.

From The Prophet, *Kahlil Gibran*

Natural Home Health Help

In the third trimester of pregnancy (30–40 weeks), the aches, pains and discomforts of pregnancy can make you feel miserable and upset. Think of them positively as the preparations that your body is making for the birth of your baby. During this time you may experience some of the following symptoms and a recurrence of some of the earlier problems already mentioned such as nausea and fatigue.

Backache

The joints of the pelvis are now beginning to loosen up to allow easier passage for your baby's delivery. This change, coupled with a larger abdomen, can throw the body off-balance with the result that you may find yourself curving your spine and waddling your hips, thus causing undue strain on the spine and back muscles. To counteract this strain, take note of the following suggestions:

• Reduce back strain with the help of your pelvic tilt exercises (see pages 26, 28, 29 and 31) and always try to keep your weight evenly distributed.

• Use the special postural exercises (see pages 22–3) to get up and down from your chair without straining.

• Don't lift abruptly – use your thighs not your back muscles when lifting.

• Sit in well-supported chairs and sleep on a firm mattress. Use more cushions for support if necessary.

• Wear comfortable shoes.

• Massage your body by giving it a good scrub in the shower or bath using a long-handled natural bristle brush. This will help your circulation.

Fluid retention (oedema)

As your baby grows and your body expands, so does the tendency to retain fluid, which is quite natural. Although the presence of oedema may indicate pre-eclampsia (a condition that can occur in late pregnancy), slightly swollen ankles, fingers and face are not necessarily cause for concern – but they may be discomforting and unhelpful for self-image.

• The third trimester is often a time when your rings can feel tight on your fingers so, if you have not done so already, remove them, put them on a chain around your neck or have them enlarged.

• It has been known for contact lenses to cause aggravation and not quite fit at this time, so perhaps you will need to revert to your glasses.

• All the Yoga programmes and self-massage techniques will help to address the general condition of oedema.

Hypertension (high blood pressure)

During pregnancy the volume of blood circulating around your body increases by 40–50 per cent. This is one of the main reasons why women feel warmer than usual and uncomfortable in very hot weather. Regular checks with your doctor will reveal whether you have a tendency to hypertension (high blood pressure).

• If your blood pressure is high, the best answer is rest – and rest means *rest*. Take your clothes off and get into bed to allow your body to breathe.

• If complete quiet and rest is not possible, try the next-best thing – listening to calming music and burning essential oils.

• Pamper yourself while you still can. Relax at length in a soothing bath and read that book that you have always wanted to read – you simply may not have enough time for such indulgences after the birth.

Itchiness

As your abdomen stretches to its maximum extent, you may suffer from itchiness. Massage, movement and putting your feet up every day are the best remedies I know for this problem, but you can also try the following.

• Oiling the skin is an excellent way to relieve or prevent itchiness.

• If the itchiness becomes very annoying, try applying camomile lotion or your best face cream (unscented).

Hair and skin problems

These are caused by an increase in oil secretion during this stage of pregnancy.

• If your hair is long and somewhat lanky, give yourself a lift by pinning it up with some pretty combs and even adding a few flowers.

• Treat dry skin on your feet by soaking them in hot water with a foot bath treatment for at least an hour. Then use a pumice stone to remove the dead skin and massage with rich face cream.

Emotional states

At all stages of pregnancy you are on show and the centre of someone's attention. This in itself can be a psychological strain, let alone the fact that you are undergoing often unfamiliar hormonal changes. Fears regarding the birth process, the future of your child and how you will cope as a parent all lead to altered states both emotionally and psychologically.

If this is your first child, trust that your baby will soon turn you into an expert mother. Make sure that you remember to practise the breathing and meditative techniques regularly. They will teach you the value of self-observation and prevent you getting too attached to any particular negative or fearful state.

The Circle of Life

In spiritual tradition the circle represents Spirit – the unbroken cycle of life from birth to death to rebirth. This is a significant symbol for women at a time when these issues are paramount. Although this sequence has a number of useful physical benefits, the significance of working with such a potent symbol of life has a positively life-affirming effect. Psychologically, I find it helps to soften the hard corners of life. So many Yoga practices seem to be angular and masculine – using the hoop and moving in an elegant, rounded, flowing, feminine manner is a wonderful complement.

This sequence is an excellent preparation for birth. Deceptively simple, it works on every joint and muscle, opening the pelvis and toning and conditioning the whole body. Not every heavily pregnant woman can sit comfortably on the floor, so I suggest you use a chair for this practice. A standard-sized plastic hoop 75–90 cm (30–36 inches) in diameter is ideal for this sequence, although you can work with an imaginary one.

There are no special contraindications to The Circle of Life sequence. Do, however, make sure you are seated securely on the front of your chair and, if necessary, secure it against the wall.

Concentration and mental awareness of a chakra or psychic energy node greatly improves the understanding and effectiveness of every posture. For this sequence your energetic focus is on the symbol of the circle. Your imaginative thought might be: **'I am connected to the circle of life.'**

[1] Sit securely on the front edge of a chair. Open your pelvis and place your feet so that your legs form a square, with the knees positioned above the ankles. With your pelvis, spine, neck and head in an upright, though not rigid, position, hold your hoop, imaginary or actual, with your elbows bent at waist level. Hold for two to three natural breaths as you work with the empowering body form and imagery.

[2] Inhale, then exhale for a count of five as you lean and stretch over to the right, bending from the waist, and making a clockwise turn of the hoop to the maximum stretch you can achieve while still keeping your buttocks firmly on the chair.
» Turn your head to look at the top of the hoop. If this is too much of a strain, then gaze down at the floor. The axis around which the hoop turns is at the level of the base of the throat and the hands should swivel naturally on the hoop's edge to accommodate the movement.
» Once you are in the final position, an extra little rotation may be possible, particularly if you decide to hold the static stretch.

1

2

[3] Inhale for a count of five as you return to the upright starting position. Exhale for a count of five as you sweep smoothly into an anticlockwise turn with a left-side bend from the waist – it is the body that does the work, not the hands. The hoop is only an aid to refine and define the movement once the stretch has been made. **»** Repeat the stretching circle at least five further times to each side.

[4] From the starting position, draw your heels and balls of the feet together, bending the knees in an open diamond shape.

[5] Inhale, then exhale for a count of five, leaning and stretching to the right as before.

[6] Inhale as you return to the new starting position, and exhale as you perform the stretching circle to your left side. Repeat the movement at least five further times to each side.

3

4

5

6

Elevator Stretch

There are all sorts of old wives' tales about how to prepare for birth. Most women have a burst of energy just before their waters break and feel a need to get the nest ready. This is all very well and rewarding, but it is equally important that you tap into your source of energy to prepare your body for the birth process. This powerful sequence will help you to connect to these vital forces by gaining control of the pelvic floor – just don't overdo this empowering practice in your enthusiasm!

Along with the elevating and descending imagery you may wish to become aware of and psychically activate, your energetic focus is on the chakras from *mooladhara chakra* (root centre) to *ajna chakra*, the Third Eye, and back again. Your imaginative thought might be:
'I have the strength, power and skill to enjoy all experiences that flow through my being.'

1

[1] Sit securely on the front edge of a chair. Open the pelvis and place your feet so that your legs form a square with your knees positioned above your ankles. Place your hands on your inner thighs just behind your knees and use them as a lever to extend your torso out of your hips and open your legs to the maximum stretch. Leaning slightly forwards, ensure that your spine, neck and head are in an upright, though not rigid, position.
» Exhale, then inhale, gently drawing the pelvic floor muscles inwards and upwards, imagining they are an elevator ascending the Empire State Building. Pause momentarily.

2

[2] Exhale slowly as you gently lower the pelvic floor muscles, imagining the elevator descending to the basement as you slide your hands down to your ankles. Repeat the sequence a further five times.

[3] From the starting position, bring your legs together, locking your ankles, knees and hips and resting on the balls of your feet. Hold the sides of the chair seat, slightly behind your hips.
» Exhale, then inhale, closing your eyes and mentally elevating the pelvic floor muscles inwards and upwards as you arch your body and head backwards to your maximum comfortable stretch. » Pause momentarily, then exhale as you lower the pelvic floor muscles as the elevator descends, and return to the starting position. Repeat the sequence a further five times.

[4] Winding down

Sit astride the chair facing the chair back and resting your forehead on your folded arms. This is also a wonderful resting position to use for the first stage of labour.

3

4

Concertina Stretch

The last stage of pregnancy can prove tiring if you don't take certain precautions. Putting your feet up is a must if you want to prevent and ease fluid retention, relieve backache and, more importantly, help to settle your emotions and keep yourself calm and centred. Make sure you do your practice supported by several firm pillows under your head, shoulders and ribcage. You will also need a chair for this sequence.

Your energetic focus is on *swadhistana chakra* (sexual centre). Your imaginative thought might be: **'I am climbing a stairway to heaven.'**

1

2

[1] Lie on the floor supporting your hips, ribcage, shoulders and head with a progressively elevating series of firm pillows, with the lowest step beneath the small of the back. Hold the legs of the chair, placing the soles of your feet together with the edges resting against the chair back.
» Open your knees into a diamond shape and open your hips to your maximum comfortable stretch. Hold for two minutes, breathing naturally.

[2] Tilt the chair back, raising the back legs of the chair as you extend your legs to shoulder-width apart to drain and relax them. Hold for one minute, breathing naturally.

[3] Exhale as you bring the chair legs back onto the floor, and concertina your knees in towards you. Inhale as you extend your legs again. Repeat the sequence a further five times.

[4] Winding down

Wind down by resting your legs on the chair seat, breathing naturally for as long as you wish.

3

4

Self-massage

Taking time out to give yourself a massage with your favourite body lotion is a must. This self-appreciation will also be felt by your baby on a subliminal level. It is important to have kept up your oiling and lotioning to prevent stretchmarks, but even if you haven't, it's not too late to start now. The massage techniques outlined here also act as a natural diuretic by working on the lymphathic system.

You can, of course, practise this self-massage while fully clothed, but why not spoil yourself by performing it unclothed after your bath or shower? If you have difficulty sleeping, practise the techniques described on pages 106–7, in bed.

With all lymphatic drainage techniques, the flow of blood should be towards the heart. Therefore your energetic focus is on *anahata chakra* (the heart centre). Your imaginative thought might be:
'Tender touch soothes my body and calms my baby.'

Safety note
If you suffer from high blood pressure, use a gentler touch when performing this massage.

[1] Sit on a chair and massage some lotion into your arms. Raise your right arm overhead, clasping your left hand around your right hand. Firmly smooth and 'drain' down your arm as if you were 'milking' the blood towards your heart. Repeat several times to ensure that you cover the whole surface of the raised arm.

1

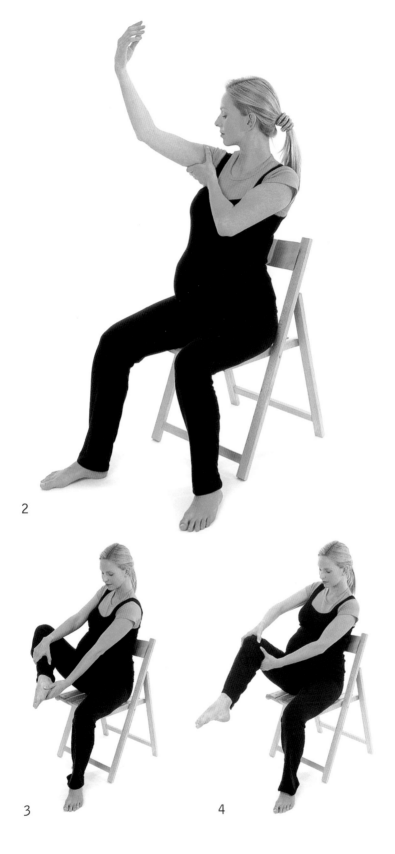

[2] Continue the draining motion into the armpit, around the outer side of the breast and into the centre of the ribcage. Repeat several times. **»** Raise the left arm and repeat the arm and torso massages. **»** Repeat the whole arm- and torso-draining sequence two further times on each side. Breathe naturally throughout.

[3] Raise and bend the right leg and, as if you were smoothing on a silk stocking, apply the lymphatic drainage technique from the toes to the front and back of the knee. Repeat several times to ensure that you cover the whole surface of the lower leg.

[4] Still breathing naturally, drain from around and behind the knee into the groin and hip. Repeat several times to ensure that you cover the whole surface of your thigh. **»** Raise your left leg and repeat the leg-draining massages. Repeat the whole leg-draining sequence two further times on each side. Breathe naturally throughout.

2

3   4

Figure-of-eight Massage

This is my favourite massage technique. The whole sequence is a fluid, crossover, figure-of-eight-style movement, reminiscent of a spring flowing through a boulder-strewn watercourse. Once again, you can perform it either with lotion on a naked body or while fully clothed. It is simple and nurturing, with the physical benefits of easing neck and shoulder tensions and smoothing away indigestion. Energetically, working on the area around *manipura chakra* (the naval centre) can help to calm the emotions. It can also be very helpful during the first stages of labour.

Your energetic focus will be on the *manipura chakra* (naval centre) and *anahata chakra* (heart centre). Your imaginative thought might be: **'Love springs eternal.'**

[1] Sit on the front edge of your chair, with your heels touching and your legs forming an open diamond shape. Cross your arms over your chest and gently clasp your hands over your neck and shoulder muscles.

[2] Keeping to a natural rhythm of breathing throughout, open your elbows as you slide your arms down, drawing on the muscles, and bringing your hands to meet at the level of the heart, one above the other.

1

2

[3]   Continuing the action, smooth both hands under your left breast and around the left side (clockwise) of your baby bump. Alternatively, you may find that by sweeping over to the right (anticlockwise) will feel more natural.

[4]   Then cradle under your baby as you move across to the right side (left side if you are working anticlockwise).

[5]   Continue moving your hands in one smooth sweep, around to the right (left) side of your baby bump, under the right (left) breast, reversing back with both hands at the heart and then crossing back up to the starting position. Repeat the whole sequence five further times.

3

4

5

Sarong Stretch I

At this stage of your pregnancy, you may begin to feel a little too restricted to perform certain movements, especially forward stretching. Hamstrings (the tendons at the back of the knee) can tighten due to chair-sitting, so I have included a mild version of the classical posture, the Back Stretching Pose (*Paschimottanasana*), which uses a sarong as an aid to make some forward progress.

This first sarong sequence will stretch the hamstrings, increase flexibility in the hip joints and tone and massage the entire abdominal and pelvic region, including all the internal organs and glands.

Your energetic focus is on *swadisthana chakra*, the sexual centre, where vitality is increased and appetite regulated. Your imaginative thought might be: **'I am harnessing the unruly senses.'**

Safety note
Do not practise the Sarong Stretch if you are recovering from, or have a history of, prolapsed disks or sciatica.

[1] Sit on the floor, bending your legs and opening your knees. Slide a folded sarong under your feet and lightly wrap the ends around your hands. Extend your legs forwards and together, taking up any slack in the sarong band. Exhale, then inhale and pull your back up to a vertical position, flexing the feet and using the sarong as leverage. **»** Exhale slowly, then hold the position for two to three natural breaths. Feel your hamstrings stretch as you pull on the sarong.

1

[2] Inhale, then exhale, easing forwards from the hips and pulling on the sarong. Push your elbows outwards and soften the knees, parting the feet slightly if necessary. **»** Hold this position momentarily, then ease back up to the starting position. Repeat six times, breathing naturally.

[3] Inhale, stretching your body upwards to a vertical position and tilting the front of the pubic bone towards the floor. Exhale and tuck the tailbone in and lean back. This is primarily the counterstretch to the forward bend, so do not overdo it. **»** Repeat the forward and backward movements of this and the previous steps six times.

[4] Fold your right foot under your left thigh to give a firm base. Cradle your left foot in the folded sarong. Inhale, lifting your leg and leaning back slightly to prevent any strain. Tilt or rotate the raised leg slightly outwards to give more leverage in the hips. Exhale and lower the leg. **»** Repeat six times on each leg. This position helps to prevent leg cramps and fluid retention.

Sarong Stretch II

There is certainly an honourable tradition of Yogis using a band to assist with meditation postures and, throughout history, women have used clothing to bind their babies around their body. Using a sarong to stretch and support your body during your pregnancy will imbue the fabric with your personal musk and energetic signature – altogether, an excellent crib comforter.

The second sequence of sarong stretches keeps the ankles, knees and hips flexible. The final winding-down position with the body bound by a sarong is a great support and relief for backache.

Your energetic focus is on *swadisthana chakra*, the sexual centre. Your imaginative thought might be:
'I grow when I push beyond what I already know.'

[1] Sit upright, placing the soles of your feet together. Form an open diamond shape with your legs, and harness your feet with the sarong. Exhale, then inhale for a count of five as you stretch yourself upwards.

[2] Exhale for a count of five as you pull your feet into your body. Hold the stretch for a short while, breathing naturally, as you ease your knees down towards the floor.

[3] Remove the sarong and place the outer side of your left foot onto the right instep. Your aim is to turn the soles of the feet upwards, one cradled by the other. Ease forwards and take your weight onto the upturned feet, opening the knees while supporting the body with the arms behind you. Hold for six natural breaths.

[4] Sit with your knees raised and ankles crossed. Bind your sarong around your middle and lower back and your shins. Knot and hold it in place with your hands. You will be able to lean back into the sarong for full and comfortable support. Your arms will also provide additional security. Hold for as long as you wish, breathing naturally.

1

2

3

4

Fancy Footwork

These classical foot positions were taught to me by Indian dancers in Kerala. The strong stretches ensure that you hold your body correctly. Correct alignment of your posture takes the pressure off your feet and will keep them beautifully flexible. Do not hold any of the movements for too long. Just momentarily pause in the position and move onto the next one.

This practice can justly be considered a self-help reflexology treatment, preventing such conditions as chilblains and cold feet.

Your energetic focus is on *mooladhara chakra*, the root centre. Your imaginative thought might be: **'I walk lightly on the earth.'**

Safety note
If you suffer from varicose veins, place a soft, rolled hand towel beneath your ankle bones and another over the top of your calves before beginning the practice.

[1] Kneel on all fours and carefully sit back onto your insteps by relaxing your heels outwards. Allow your knees to part naturally. Hold the position for two to three natural breaths, resting your hands lightly on your lap.

1

2

[2] Come back onto all fours and cross the top of the right foot into the left instep, relaxing your heels outwards. Sit back down into the position, correcting your posture into one of natural alignment. Place your hands lightly in your lap and rest for two to three natural breaths. **»** Rise up onto your knees again as you exchange feet positions so that your left foot is over the right instep. Sit back down into the position and hold for a further two to three natural breaths.

[3] Rise up onto all fours and, keeping your knees together, flex your feet and lock your ankles. Sit back down onto your heels and hold the position for two to three natural breaths.

[4] Rise up onto all fours again, taking the weight on your hands. Open your feet and sit down onto a large, firm, rolled bath towel. Hold for two to three natural breaths. **»** If the previous sequence has not proved too taxing for your feet, repeat two further times, trying to sit on the floor between the feet without the rolled towel in the final position. At all times, be sure to take the body's weight on your hands before sitting down, to avoid any strain on your knees.

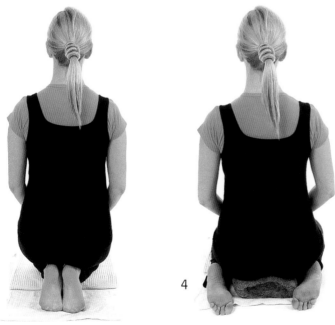

3   4

Programme Twelve

Bamboo Workout

I have developed this bamboo stick workout over some years. It contains elements of the Egyptian, Indian and African stick-fighting and martial arts training routines. You will require a piece of bamboo or broom handle dowelling approximately the length of your arm from wrist to shoulder. It is surprising how using a straight stick – very much a masculine symbol – leads to smooth, circular and continuously flowing motions that spiral around the body and are very feminine in nature. You can perform the sequence dynamically and energetically as a physical toning aid for the whole body, or in a more meditative way as a beautiful dance.

The workout eases and flexes the main axles of the body – the shoulders, elbows, wrists, hips, knees and ankles.

Your energetic focus is on the whole chakra system. Your imaginative thought might be: **'I am the mistress of myself.'**

[1] Stand with your legs comfortably apart, resting the bamboo stick lightly on your upturned palms.

[2] Inhale, then exhale, bending your knees as you offer your right hand to the earth, honouring its energies. Keep your head up if you suffer from high blood pressure.

[3] Inhale, straightening your legs, and turning the bamboo over on its end so that the right hand touches your heart, making the energetic connection, as your left arm extends forwards.

[4] Drop your right hand as you rotate your extended left arm around to the right, threading your right elbow through the gap.

[5] Continue inhaling with the movement as, with a flowing motion, the bamboo stick circles upwards behind the back. Raise your arms until the left hand is above the crown of the head and the bamboo is vertically suspended behind your back.

[6] Exhale as you lower your left hand down to waist level, keeping the right hand in place behind your back.

[7] Continue exhaling as you rotate your body 90 degrees to the right, swivelling on your feet. Bend until your left knee touches the ground. The bamboo stick sweeps round and points in the direction you are facing.
» Pause momentarily, then inhale as you unwind and reverse the sequence until you regain the starting position. Repeat the sequence in mirror fashion, with the left hand leading the movements. This completes one round. **»** Repeat the whole sequence for a further five rounds.

1

2

3

4A

4B

5

6A

6B

7

Lotus Lily Dance I

Through years of fine-tuning, I have developed this sequence (pages 116–9) from a simple story I enacted for my own children at their first Yoga class. The Lotus Lily Dance represents the life cycle of the lotus. The flower has always been a symbol of spiritual growth, coming out of the darkness of mud, through the medium of water eventually to bloom in the air and sunlight. In Yogic and Tantric texts, the chakras of the subtle and energetic body are often referred to as 'lotuses'.

This form of moving meditation or sacred dance is very much part of the culture of pregnant women in India who harmonize their mind and body during labour by focusing on an image of a lotus flower. As the petals slowly unfold, the woman imagines her cervix opening with each contraction, helping to make a safe pathway for her baby to travel through into the waiting world.

What you get out of the dance will very much depend on the attitude with which you approach it. It is even possible, like the gifted sacred dancers, to achieve a state of transcendence of the ordinary – 'To see a World in a grain of sand, and Heaven in a wild flower, hold Infinity in the palm of your hand, and Eternity in an hour.' (William Blake)

Your imaginative thought might be:
'I am a flower, opening to perfection in the light of the sun.'

[1] *The Lotus Lily starts her day in stillness.*

» Stand with your legs comfortably apart, palms cupped in a bud shape at the heart centre. Breathe naturally throughout the sequence.

[2] *As the sun comes up, she opens her petals. By midday, her face is smiling in the sunshine.*

» Bending your knees into an easy diamond shape, move your hands slowly upwards, bringing your elbows together. Open your hands and wrists outwards to form the petals of the opening flower. Tilt your head upwards and backwards.

[3] *The gentle breeze sways her to the right.*

» Close your hands and draw them back to the heart like petals gently closing. Slide your left hand down your right forearm until your middle finger touches your right elbow. Turn the palm of your hand outwards and bend into the movement, leaning over to the right with your head turned to face to the left. Your arms, both curving outwards, form a gentle arch.

[4] *The breeze sways her to the left.*

» Return to the centre and slide your right hand down the left arm as you mirror your posture to the opposite side.

1

2

3

4

Lotus Lily Dance II

The second part of the Lotus Lily Dance involves a certain amount of mime and mimicry which are a delight to young children. Perhaps, in time, you will teach it to your baby.

5

[5] *Many tiny fish swim in a figure-of-eight around her roots.*

» Place one palm on top of the other, thumbs extended. Rotate the thumbs to propel the fish through the water as you inscribe a figure-of-eight from left to right, bending the knees as if descending to the bottom of the pool.

[6] *The air is alive with jewelled butterflies and singing birds.*

» Put your arms out to your side and let your hands mimic butterfly wings as your arms gently flap like the wings of a slow-flying bird.

[7] *As dusk gathers, the Lotus Lily closes her petals, sealing in the inspiration of the day.*

» Bring your palms together above your head on gently extended arms.

[8] *She rests peacefully until dawn.*

» Cradle your hands under your baby, using a classical *mudra* with the thumb tips touching and the fingers of one hand resting on the other.

» Repeat the whole sequence as often as you wish, synchronizing with your breathing as you become more familiar with the dance.

6

7

8

Birth Breathing

The following description of the stages of labour illustrates the vital importance of deep relaxation, breathing techniques and visualization. Candle and Feather Breathing elegantly emphasize the need to prolong the outgoing breath, and will help you keep calm at a time when it is easy to lose control. Your Yoga practices can assist your baby's safe delivery and ease much of the discomfort caused by fear and tension.

Relaxation: first stage of labour

Your main focus during the beginning of the first stage of labour should be on relaxation (see *Yoga Nidra*, pages 20–1) with imagery to assist your breathing processes. **»** Focus on the out-breath during a contraction, that is breathing out for as long as you can through a soft mouth. Imagine that you are inhaling a cooling natural painkiller from the environment, administering it to the painful area and then mentally breathing out the heat of discomfort. Although it is vital to listen to what your body is telling you during labour, at this stage you will have to do something that does not seem natural. At the end of the first stage, as the contractions are really building up, your inclination will be to inhale as the pain starts; what you really need to do is breathe *out* and let go. Breathe as deeply as is comfortable.

Feather Breathing

You may find that as the contractions increase in intensity you need to breathe more shallowly at the height of each contraction. You may find it helpful to imagine that you have a feather on the palm of your hand and you are gently moving it as you exhale. Another image that may help is to imagine the breath as a little boat that you lift on the wave of discomfort and ride until the pain subsides. Alternatively, as you breathe out as the contraction begins, imagine a ripple of relaxation on a calm pond. Let the ripple travel through the muscles of your shoulders, chest, abdomen, pelvic floor and legs. Follow this by breathing comfortably and calmly throughout the contraction. **»** Between contractions, take some deep refreshing and relaxing breaths, and remember that you are another contraction nearer to meeting your baby. Don't hold or force your breath – listen to your body for the impulse to breathe. This will come naturally if you avoid panicking. Much will depend on your mental attitude and focus. A soft mouth and lips are the ideal gauge to your progress. The tighter the lips, the tighter the pelvic floor; the softer the lips the softer the pelvic floor area.

Candle Breathing: transition period

For some women there is a transition period at the end of the first stage, when the cervix has not yet fully dilated. It is important at this time that you control the natural impulse to push. The short puffing breaths of Candle Breathing may help. Imagine the fingers of one hand are little lighted candles on your baby's birthday cake. **»** When the pushing urge comes, exhale with short puffs, extinguishing the flames one by one. Alternatively, use the words: 'I – must – not – push ... I – must – not – push ...' (using short exhalations for each word and short inhalations between, with a longer exhalation on 'push').

Working with your body

During the second stage of labour, the pushing urges become stronger and you can no longer resist them. There may be several pushing urges within one contraction, so it is important to listen to what your body is telling you to do. When you feel the pushing urge, inhale, hold the breath momentarily as you steady yourself, then breathe out with a long, slow but strong breath as your body gently eases the baby down the birth canal. **»** Between pushing urges, keep your breathing light and your mouth soft in order to relax the pelvic floor. With the next pushing urge, again hold your breath momentarily, gently pushing down on the diaphragm as you release the breath through your mouth. Breathe lightly between urges, focus on relaxing the pelvic floor and remember that each breath is bringing you closer to holding your baby in your arms. **»** Between contractions, take deep relaxing and refreshing breaths, breathing in energy to help you through the next contraction. The essential points to remember here are to get yourself into a comfortable position which suits you and which will ease your baby's passage into our world; to remain relaxed by focusing on allowing your body to soften and open up for the baby; to listen to what your body is asking of you; and to keep your lips and jaw soft and your breathing comfortable and unhurried.

Your baby's arrival: delivery

When you reach this point, you may get several urges to push in one contraction and a good midwife will guide you through, so do listen to what you're being told. Just before your baby is born you will be asked to pant. Your uterus will push the baby out irrespective of what you do, but you can help the process. Your final thought is: '*It's not how much breath I can take in, it's how much I can let go with a calm and focused mind.*'

Greeting your baby

Once your baby is in your arms, for you the hard work of labour is over. This is not the case for the midwife: she still has to oversee the birth of the placenta, your baby's life-support system. You may be aware of mild contractions at this point and may be asked to give another push. For you these events may pass almost unnoticed as you begin to take in

the reality of the small bundle of a wonderful new life and a new beginning that you cradle in your arms.

Right: Feather Breathing.
Below: Candle Breathing.

Candle Meditation

The word *Trataka* means to gaze steadily. This meditation involves gazing at a candle and is one of the best-known of the meditational practices. It can safely be practised at any time during pregnancy. *Trataka* will develop your powers of concentration, a prerequisite to all meditational practices, improve memory, rectify eye defects and alleviate insomnia. Women have gazed into fire and flames since the dawn of time, and healers and sensitives, particularly, have used it to access the psychic realms. The practice is quite safe and can be an excellent method for clearing accumulated complexes, problems and suppressed thoughts. However, if this is too disturbing for you, rather than enlightening, discontinue the practice and seek expert help from a teacher.

Place a lighted candle on a small table approximately at arm's length away from you and at eye level. Sit in a comfortable meditational sitting position (see Postures for Seated Meditation, pages 90–1), supporting yourself with a cushion or meditation stool if necessary. Alternatively, sit in a straight-backed chair with your head, neck and spine in alignment.

Close your eyes and relax completely. Open your eyes and gaze steadily at the tip of the wick. Try not to blink or move the eyeballs in any way. This may take some practice and you must carefully monitor yourself in the early stages. Do not strain your face or furrow your brow: concentration is an inner attribute, not an outward expression. Ultimately your awareness will be so centred on the candle flame that you will lose awareness of your physical body. » If your mind starts to wander, gently bring it back to the practice. When, after a few minutes, your eyes become tired and start to water, gently close them. You will then see the after-image retained on the retina for some time. Keep your concentration on the image, endeavouring to keep it stable in your mind's eye. Once the image has completely disappeared, open your eyes and gaze once more at the candle flame. Complete this process two or three times, then more frequently after regular practice. » At the end of your practice, internally repeat this aspirational thought: **'There is a healing light shining in the centre of my being.'**

Miracle Day

*'I saw your face. I touched your hand. I held your
body and we fell in love.'*

Rosalind Widdowson

Bibliography

The following books were invaluable during the research phase and some have been old friends for many years. I can wholeheartedly recommend every one of them.

Eisenberg, Murkoff and Hathaway. 'What to Expect when you're Expecting', Simon and Schuster, 1996

Enkin, Keirse and Chalmers. 'A Guide to Effective Care in Pregnancy and Childbirth', Oxford University press Inc., USA, 2000

Gibran, Kahlil. 'The Prophet', Pan Books (Macmillan), 1991

Iyengar, B.K.S. 'Light on Pranayama', George, Allen and Unwin, London, 1981

Iyengar, B.K.S. 'Light on Yoga', George, Allen and Unwin, London, 1966

Kitzinger, Sheila. 'Pregnancy and Childbirth', Penguin Books, 1997

Kitzinger, Sheila. 'Pregnancy, Birth & Parenthood'

'Mamatoto – A Celebration of Birth', The Body Shop

Nolan, Mary. 'Being Pregnant, Giving Birth', The National Childbirth Trust

Priya, Jacqueline Vincent. 'Birth Traditions and Modern Pregnancy Care', Element Books Ltd, 1992

Shapiro, Eddie and Debbie (eds). 'The Way Ahead', Element Books Ltd, 1992

Silva, Mira and Shyam, Mehta. 'Yoga the Iyengar Way', Dorling Kindersley, London, 1990

Stewart, Mary. 'Yoga Over 50', Little, Brown & Company, London, 195

Sunita, Yogini. 'Pranayama Yoga – The Art of Relaxation'

Swami Satyananda Saraswati. 'Tantra of Kundalini Yoga'

Swami Satyananda Saraswati. 'Yoga Nidra'

Swami Satyananda Saraswati. 'Asana, Pranayama, Mudra, Bandha'

The Sivananda Yoga Centre. 'The Book of Yoga', Gaia Books, London, 1993

Widdowson, Rosalind. 'Easy Steps to Relaxation and Meditation', Grange Books, London, 1995

Widdowson, Rosalind. 'Easy Steps to Natural Healing', Grange Books, London, 1995

Widdowson, Rosalind. 'Easy Steps to Aromatherapy', Grange Books, London, 1995

Widdowson, Rosalind. 'Easy Steps to Massage', Grange Books, London, 1995

Widdowson, Rosalind. 'Yoga made Easy', Newnes Books (Hamlyn), 1983

Index

Acknowledgements

The process of writing any book stretches back through the years even to the earliest and most formative experiences. In respect and gratitude for all I have learnt about Yoga and dance, I offer my thanks to my teachers: Lettie, my Afro-Indian nanny in South Africa; Audrey Biggs; Vilma Henwood; Betty Fox; B.K.S. Iyengar; Yogini Sunita; Wilfred Clark; H.H. Swami Sivananda Saraswati; Paramahansa Satyananda; my beloved co-writer Swami Tantramurti Saraswati for all his loving support; and to every single one of my students. They have taught me so much and continue to be the very best advocates and examples of the inspiration and benefits that Yoga can bestow on all humankind.

For their very kind help on the preshoot in Thailand, I wish to thank Dr John Towell, Suzanne Grundy, Alice Mortimer and my dear friend and photographer, Sam Southall; for the final London shoot, Andy at Blank Space, photographer Peter Pugh-Cooke and the charming models Claire Ford, Susan Alston, Rachel Patrick, Anneka Svenska and Sylvia Bazzarelli and their beautiful bumps; and at Hamlyn for all their faith, help and kindness in making this such a special project, Jane McIntosh and Claire Harvey.

Finally, special thanks go to my new friend Carol Pannell (B Ed) who is an antenatal expert and teacher as well as an advanced teacher/assessor for the National Childbirth Trust. She has given unstintingly of her time, great expertise and wisdom in gestating this book.